FILM FOCUS

Ronald Gottesman and Harry M. Geduld
General Editors

THE FILM FOCUS SERIES PRESENTS THE BEST THAT HAS BEEN
WRITTEN ABOUT THE ART OF FILM AND THE MEN WHO CREATED
IT. COMBINING CRITICISM WITH HISTORY, BIOGRAPHY, AND ANAL-
YSIS OF TECHNIQUE, THE VOLUMES IN THE SERIES EXPLORE THE
MANY DIMENSIONS OF THE FILM MEDIUM AND ITS IMPACT ON
MODERN SOCIETY.

JACK NACHBAR *divides his time between the English Depart-
ment and the Center for the Study of Popular Culture at
Bowling Green State University, where he teaches courses in
American literature, Shakespeare, popular culture, and
movies. He reviews films weekly for local radio and television and is co-editor of the quarterly* Journal of Popular
Film.

ACKNOWLEDGMENTS

For their help, suggestions and encouragement in the preparation of this volume, special thanks are hereby given to the following people: Ronald Gottesman for his initial and continuing interest and his suggestions for materials; all my colleagues at the Center for the Study of Popular Culture, especially Ray B. Browne, Sam Grogg, Jr. and Michael Marsden for hours of useful discussion and for specific suggestions on materials; Mary Corliss of the Museum of Modern Art for valuable advice; Jon Tuska and Kathryn Esselman for helpful suggestions and corrections of the chronology; Garth Jowett, Larry Landrum and the staff of the American Film Institute, especially Anne G. Schlosser for providing materials essential in preparing the bibliography; and, finally, Lynn Nachbar for her many hours of help in gathering and editing materials and for the continuous encouragement of her marvelous enthusiasm for Westerns.

FOCUS ON

THE WESTERN

◆◇◆

edited by

JACK NACHBAR

A SPECTRUM BOOK

Prentice-Hall, Inc.
Englewood Cliffs, N. J.

Library of Congress Cataloging in Publication Data

NACHBAR, JACK, COMP.
 Focus on the western.

 (Film focus) (A Spectrum Book)
 CONTENTS: Nachbar, J. Introduction.—Esselman, K. C.
From Camelot to Monument Valley.—Etulain, R. W.
Cultural origins of the western. [etc.]
  1. Western films—Addresses, essays, lectures.
I. Title.
PN1995.9.W4N3   016.79143   74-3063
ISBN 0-13-950634-9
ISBN 0-13-950626-8 (pbk.)

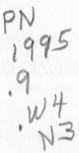

PN
1995
.9
.W4
.N3

Printed in the United States of America

10   9   8   7   6   5   4   3   2   1

PRENTICE-HALL INTERNATIONAL, INC. (*London*)
PRENTICE-HALL OF AUSTRALIA, PTY. LTD. (*Sydney*)
PRENTICE-HALL OF CANADA, LTD. (*Toronto*)
PRENTICE-HALL OF INDIA PRIVATE LIMITED (*New Delhi*)
PRENTICE-HALL OF JAPAN, INC. (*Tokyo*)

CONTENTS

THE WESTERN AS
CULTURAL ARTIFACT

THE CONTEMPORARY
WESTERN

Introduction
by JACK NACHBAR

It's now a quarter of a century since Westerns took up my whole life. There were, first of all, in those pleasant postwar years in Minneapolis, endless summer hours of "playing cowboys." Whenever it rained we read or traded our Western comic books. I remember especially liking Monte Hale and "Rocky" Lane comics because their movies never came to our theater. Three times a week supper was bolted to catch "The Lone Ranger" on the radio. All these activities, of course, were just killing time, trivial warm-ups for Saturdays, when we would gather an hour before the box office opened in front of the Nokomis Theater, only three blocks away, in order to be the first neighborhood bunch to shove our twelve cents at the cashier and have our choice of seats to watch a Western serial, invariably featuring Zorro or the James Brothers, and to see a matinee Western, with Johnny Mack Brown or Sunset Carson, whom we disliked, or Charles Starrett, Whip Wilson, or Hopalong Cassidy, whom we liked or, on very special days, Roy Rogers, who was always shown with ten extra cartoons and whom every one of us adored. Sometimes we would be lucky and the regular feature would also be a Western like *Colorado Territory* with Joel McCrae or *Fighting Man of the Plains* with Randolph Scott, which we would always sit through twice, making our time at the Saturday movies about eight hours, not a second of which ever occurred to us was useless or wasted or boring. So predictably ritualistic were the gunplay, fistfights and riding on the screen and so religious was my attendance that once, when I got to the theater a few minutes late and alone to see *Calamity Jane and Sam Bass*, I unthinkingly betrayed my Catholic school upbringing and genuflected by the side of my seat. I saw nothing incongruous about this until a couple of my pals told each other out loud what I'd done and began to giggle. None of this ever struck me as in any way "meaningful." It was simply what I liked to do and what every-

---

NOTE: References with a single asterisk will be found in the bibliography. A double asterisk denotes a selection in this book.

1

body I knew liked to do. It was not until long into my adulthood that it occurred to me that it was because of the very ordinariness of my boyhood cowboymania that Westerns were significant, that the same Saturday ritual commonly experienced by millions of children and adults in thousands of theaters in all parts of the country for three generations hinted at something important about the collective mind of twentieth-century America.

Risking the charge of overstatement, Westerns, especially Western movies, are thus far the single most important American story form of the twentieth century. Consider, for example, how Westerns have dominated and influenced the U.S. film industry. Edwin S. Porter's one-reel *The Great Train Robbery* (1903) was not only the first narrative Western, but was also the U.S.'s first big box-office hit. When the first nickelodion opened in Pittsburgh in 1905 its initial attraction was *The Great Train Robbery* and the successful combination of broad physical action and the suspense of the chase that characterized *The Great Train Robbery* has come to characterize most American movies since. "Broncho Billy" Anderson, the screen's first Western hero, was the first performer to have his name be the central attraction of the movies in which he appeared. From Anderson therefore came that bedrock of Hollywood production, the "star system." Hollywood itself owes its status as the American Mount Olympus largely to the needs of Western film production. Richard Dale Batman in "The Founding of the Motion Picture Industry" * points out that the first film companies to migrate to California—Selig, Bison, Essanay, and Biograph—went, not as popularly believed, to escape prosecution for patent violations, but because California offered good shooting weather and because its scenery offered perfect locations in which to film Westerns. Finally, before television in the mid-1950's gunned down one of the staples of Hollywood security, the cheaply made "B" feature, Westerns were overwhelmingly the most prolific of American movies, most years comprising between 25 and 30 percent of American-made features. Garth Jowett points out that even during the 1950's, when the feature production of Westerns was dramatically dropping off, Westerns still comprised one-half of American made historical films.*
   It is little wonder that, because they have been so popular, so almost unavoidable, Westerns came to define for all classes of white Americans their traditional ethics, values and sources of national pride. It was appropriate, for example, when John Wayne created an ideological defense of the Vietnam War in *The Green Berets* (1968) that Western imagery helped carry the political message. The Green Beret outpost is named Dodge City. Only a bit more surprising are bits of casually reported news that demonstrate that Westerns still hold the imagination of some of the world's elite. Henry Kissinger confessed to Italian re-

porter Oriana Fallaci in 1972 that the source of his charisma while negotiating the Vietnam settlement was his being analogous to American Western heroes riding into town to face the baddies alone. The image of the negotiations, Kissinger concluded, was "a Wild West tale, if you like." [1] A similar response occurred in the summer of 1973 at the Nixon-Brezhnev summit. At one point in the meetings, as the Russian and American leaders flew over the Grand Canyon, Nixon asked Brezhnev if he had ever seen such country. NBC News showed Brezhnev answering that Yes, he had seen such scenes—in John Wayne Westerns. The two world leaders grinned at one another in what was obviously a pleasurably shared remembrance and then playfully began making the gestures of the stereotyped movie gunfight.

Several of the articles in this anthology demonstrate that the central image in Western movies is the European-American's three-centuries-long confrontation with the immense North American frontier. This relationship between the new land and the European, and the results of that relationship, were seminally defined by historian Frederick Jackson Turner in 1893 in a paper he presented before the American Historical Association entitled "The Significance of the Frontier in American History." American development, argued Turner, is explained by "an existence of an area of free land, its continuous recession, and the advance of American settlement Westward." Turner concluded that as the European continually confronted the land on an imaginary line between frontier and civilization, the experience tempered traditional European ideas of interdependent social classes and autocratic government toward American ideals of individualism, classlessness and democracy. The validity of the Turner thesis has been questioned by some historians who cite the realities of cold historical data. But its acceptance for several decades after its initial presentation as the definitive interpretation of American development demonstrates that Americans desired and believed it to be true. Turner did not define American history so much as he defined for European-Americans the central myth of their history. At the same time the Turner thesis was most universally accepted, Western movies attained their greatest popularity. The relationship is in part coincidental. Kathryn Esselman** and Richard Etulain** both show how Westerns evolved from specific popular forms and cultural attitudes around the turn of the nineteenth century. Nevertheless the relationship between the Turner thesis and Westerns is an intimate one. Turner announced in his paper that the primal American experience was over; as of 1890, census reports showed that the frontier was officially closed. Western movies, with their historical time customarily fixed between 1860 and 1890 and their location in the sparsely settled areas West of the

[1] "Kissinger." *New Republic*, December 16, 1972, p. 21.

Mississippi, are thus a perpetual re-enactment of the last moments of the white man's settlement of the wild American landscape. Just as Turner cited facts, dates and other historical data to define the essential American experience, nearly all of the thousands of Western films symbolically celebrate that experience by ritualistically recreating its essence over and over in dramas depicting in heroic terms the civilizing of the final American frontier. Besides their importance as an influence on the American film industry, Westerns have, even more crucially, affected American thought by perpetuating a psychic confidence and belief in the myth of American national identity, as defined by Frederick Jackson Turner, for more than half a century after Turner himself declared as finished forever the possibility of physically renewing that identity on new American frontiers.

II

The critical thrust of the first in-depth studies of Western movies, published in France in the early 1950's, recognized Westerns, in the words of André Bazin, as "The American Film Par Excellence," and found them praiseworthy chiefly for having accurately dramatized the essence of American frontier history.[2] This same emphasis on the value of historical accuracy was also the position of the first (1962) book-length study of Westerns published in the United States, George F. Fenin and William K. Everson's *The Western: From Silents to Cinerama*, which, because of its exhaustive references to specific films and dates, is still the most authoritative and influential book on the subject in English. The touchstone for quality Westerns for Fenin and Everson was the "realism" of the treeless landscapes, and mountains of choking dust in the films of William S. Hart. The "musical" or "singing cowboy" pictures of Gene Autry and Roy Rogers were, conversely, the low points on the Western yardstick because musical production numbers and superfancy clothes made a mockery of the West as it really was.

Westerns may indeed be American history, as Jim Kitses points out in "The Western: Ideology and Archetype," ** but history provides Westerns with no more than their "mores and milieu." The "real" West is only the physical environment of Western movies; at their heart Westerns present the "idea" of the West, history not as it in fact occurred but how it is imagined to have occurred. The danger of the

---

[2] For two illustrations in English of this French critical stance toward Westerns, see Jean-Louis Rieupeyrout's article "The Western: A Historical Genre" in Vol. 7 (1952) *of Quarterly of Film, Radio and Television,* * and André Bazin's "The Western or the American Film Par Excellence," in his *What Is Cinema, Vol. II* (Berkeley: University of California Press, 1971*).

insistence on historical fidelity posited by the French critics and by
Fenin and Everson is that Westerns will be judged upon false criteria.
Looking at a William S. Hart feature now, for example, one can still
greatly admire the allegorical directness of his imagery and the rough
integrity of Hart himself, but even Fenin and Everson admit that his
plots are filled with a Victorian sentimentality that today often seems
absurd. Hart's Westerns, as Jon Tuska points out in "The Western
Cinema: 1903–Present" ** have the same conventional plots and landscapes as most of the other Westerns of Hart's era. They have, in reality, little more historical validity than the Westerns of Autry and
Rogers. All of them represented and celebrated for their own time the
"idea" of the West as defined by Frederick Jackson Turner, Hart for
the strait-laced movie patrons of the pre-1920's, Autry for the fantasy-
starved depression audiences of the 1930's and Rogers, with his boyish
looks and "family" of secondary players, for a forties audience that
patronized movies like *Meet Me in St. Louis* and longed for images
of normalcy. To cite another example, Vidor's 1930 *Billy the Kid*,
David Miller's 1941 *Billy the Kid*, Arthur Penn's 1957 *The Left-
Handed Gun* and Sam Peckinpah's 1973 *Pat Garrett and Billy the Kid*
all misrepresent the historic William Bonney, but seeing them will aid
in understanding the changing myth of the rebel-hero playing out his
string in a landscape able to contain both the best and worst of the
rebel-hero's dialectic personality.

   The essays in this anthology were selected because they present an alternative to the assumption that Westerns should recreate history.
Each essay develops in a slightly different way the idea that Westerns
are, again, not artifacts of actual history but of the American idealiza-
tion of its history. Of special thematic value in articulating the bases
of this critical position are the essays by John Cawelti, Robert Warshow and Jim Kitses. Cawelti's monograph, *The Six-Gun Mystique*,*
is thus far the most detailed study of the Western formula. In the portion of the monograph reprinted here, "Savagery, Civilization and the
Western Hero," ** Cawelti defines a Western as a re-enactment of an
American "epic moment" when the settler faced the West and, fighting
it desperately for survival, ultimately tamed and controlled it. Warshow's 1954 "The Westerner," with its beautiful, poetic prose, is probably the most influential essay on the subject yet written. His famous
definition of the Western hero as "the last gentleman" perhaps needs
some revision in light of some of the dubious activities of the protagonists of post-1960 pictures, but his idea that the hero acts primarily
for his own personal honor rather than for the good of the community
still seems altogether valid and adds a fascinating touch of complexity
to the personality of even the most untaintedly virtuous B-Western
hero. Warshow's giving artistic merit to those films where the hero
recognizes that his code can only be maintained by violence seems to

me to be the best clue yet as to the difference between "kiddie" and "adult" Westerns. Kitses' article explains the great attraction of the Western by describing its environment in a Turner-like way as a place allowing the freedom of endless "open options." Kitses also describes the great variety of forms in which Westerns appear, thereby warning against a too-narrow interpretation of the Western-as-artifact that in its own way would be as serious a critical misjudgment as the insistence that Westerns be accurate history.

John Wayne's three-hour *The Alamo* (1960) and the lavish cinerama *How the West Was Won* (1963) were the last epic movies to unashamedly celebrate the Turner thesis. In 1962 *The Man Who Shot Liberty Valance, Lonely Are the Brave* and *Ride the High Country* all presented Western heroes performing last acts of honor and courage, but then giving in to the orderly omnipresence of civilization. With these three pictures, the Western film tradition formally called a halt to the celebration and admitted that whether or not Turner had been correct in defining the American experience, he was certainly correct in announcing its demise—the frontier and the freedom that accompanied it were indeed no more. The essays in the "Contemporary Western" section describe the film trends that have resulted from this admission. All three essays seem to agree generally that most notable contemporary Westerns are either elegiac or revisionist. They are elegiac, as I point out in "Riding Shotgun: The Scattered Formula in Contemporary Western Movies," ** because Cawelti's "epic moment" has moved forward past the last days of the free frontier and, as Ralph Brauer** demonstrates, Kitses' "open options" have closed. Self-criticism, undoubtedly in part a response to the social upheavals of the 1960's, admits that blithely to celebrate the European conquest of the West is to ignore the important implications for the national character of the racism, barbarism and ecological destructiveness that accompanied it. John Cawelti's "Reflections on the New Western Films" ** shows how this self-criticism is reflected in greater sex, violence and authoritarianism. All three essays agree that contemporary Westerns are groping for a new myth of the American experience, one which might include an admission of past sins and an acknowledgment that the end of the frontier has been reached. Brauer, himself a representative of the skeptical post-Kennedy generation, as a fitting conclusion to the collection of essays voices the strong hope that such a myth may be on the Western horizon, just over the next hill.

The chronology and bibliography that conclude the anthology follow the method of the articles in presenting an overview of Westerns rather than concentrating on specific films, stars or directors. The chronology will no doubt upset any true Western fan who has his/her own favorites. Its intent is not necessarily to list the best Westerns but to present historically significant and influential films and events. The bibliography is highly selective, generally listing only those materials which discuss Westerns as a genre. A longer checklist of books, magazines and articles on Westerns, including materials on specific films and directors, appears in the Fall, 1973, issue of *The Journal of Popular Film.*

III

Frederick Jackson Turner presented his thesis in 1893 to the American Historical Association, which was meeting that year inside the grounds of the Columbian Exposition in Chicago. It is said that while Turner spoke before his fellow historians, Buffalo Bill Cody, whose Wild West Show had not been allowed on the Exposition grounds, was presenting his Indians, cowboys, horses and covered wagons to sellout crowds only a few blocks away.[3] By an uncanny coincidence, Turner, the seminal articulator of the American myth, and Cody, the nineteenth century's foremost embodiment of that myth, were thus nearly within hailing distance of one another in a city on the great prairie which more than any other symbolized the center, the heart of America, at an Exposition that symbolized the beginnings of modern America, and neither saw the other, nor, probably, knew or cared that the other was there. As much as *Stagecoach* and *Shane* are archetypes of white America's taking of the land, that moment of two great men converging at such a culturally important crossroads but ignoring one another is an archetype for American cultural studies. The continuing pattern, until recently, has been one in which historians, social scientists and students of the humanities passed over the work, customs and entertainment of the masses as trivial and, for most part, insignificant. It was not until Turner's presentation of his thesis, for example, that most historians even began to acknowledge an element of cultural significance in the three-centuries-long settlement of the frontier. It is not surprising that the crudity of the first movies, including Westerns, made them intellectually suspect and therefore that, with the exception of a few sociologists who worried that movies were destroying the morals of American children, the educated left movies to the recent immigrants, the poor and the young.

Developments of the last twenty-five years lead to the hopeful conclusion that, at least in the study of the American frontier, heirs of the popular tradition of Buffalo Bill and the intellectual tradition of Turner may finally begin talking to one another. Scholars such as those

[3] Archie H. Jones, "Cops, Robbers, Heroes and Anti-Heroines: The American Need to Create." *Journal of Popular Culture,* I:2 (Fall, 1967), pp. 114–18.

mentioned by Richard Etulain are detailing the rich importance of such popular materials as Puritan Indian captivity narratives, dime novels and pulp magazines. On the other hand, sincere fans of Westerns, such as the Western Collectors of America, are apparently becoming more aware that Western films are historically significant artifacts and are meticulously gathering accurate data and compiling detailed filmographies about B-Western stars and Western subgenres such as "trio-Westerns" and Western serials.

There were virtually no substantive publications on Western films prior to 1950; little was done in English before the 1960's. Recent film criticism concentrating on movie genres rather than directors, and scholarship centering on the cultural analysis of films means, however, that Westerns may at last begin to receive the serious intellectual attention they long ago earned by their crucial status in the Hollywood film industry and their metaphorical and ritual presence in the mass American mind. The loss in early film material already has been tragic. Sam Kula, former archivist of the American Film Institute, estimates that less than 20 percent of silent films are still in existence. Because Westerns were so similar and so abundant, and therefore so expendable, their percentage of loss is probably even higher. Most of the great early stars are dead. Before other major losses to Western film study occur, intensive studies of Western films crucially need to be undertaken. Since Fenin and Everson's history, other volumes, including in the 1970's those by Frank Manchel * and Michael Parkinson and Clyde Jeavons,* have relied on Fenin and Everson not only for historical data but also for critical judgments. New historical studies are needed based on fresh research and more recently uncovered data.[4] While the psychological and cultural milieus of horror films and *film noir* are receiving growing critical attention, as of this writing no comprehensive cultural history of Westerns has yet appeared.

Westerns, by their sheer omnipresence were the center of my life and of the life of the entire nation twenty-five years ago. In many ways, through their continuing ability to reflect current social and political attitudes, they still are. Hopefully, the gathering together of the materials in this anthology may help gain for Western films the intensive critical attention they deserve, and for America some of the truth about itself which it so badly needs.

---

[4] As this book was being prepared for publication, Fenin and Everson's revised edition of *The Western: From Silents to Cinerama* appeared as *The Western: From Silents to The Seventies.**

ORIGINS AND DEVELOPMENT

From Camelot to Monument Valley:
Dramatic Origins of the Western Film
by KATHRYN C. ESSELMAN

The image of the knight and the concept of the quest are reflected in the American Western. The filmed Western, because of its visual nature and defined iconography, incorporates material from the Arthurian tradition and its descendants the romance and the melodrama. The connection becomes explicit in the self-conscious structuring of a film like George Stevens' *Shane* according to Arthurian modes. The television series "Have Gun, Will Travel" expressed the creator's familiarity with this tradition when the leading character was named Paladin and his trademark was a chess knight.

The knight, the quest, Camelot and, to a lesser degree, Courtly Love bear directly and indirectly on the history of the Western. The modern cowboy here became defined through a process of wedding the traditional frontiersman to the knight while visually defining him according to the conventions set by Buffalo Bill's Wild West Show and the Western melodramas. Exposure to the Arthuriad amplified the prototype created by James Fenimore Cooper in Natty Bumppo.

Arthurian romances maintained their popularity throughout the late Middle Ages, but interest declined toward the end of the sixteenth century until, by the beginning of the seventeenth century, they existed only as kitchen romances—the equivalent of modern comic books for the kitchen maids. At the turn of the nineteenth century the rise of Romanticism brought with it an awakening of interest in the ancient history of Britain. The tales of Arthur, which had met with little interest in the rationalist climate of the past two hundred years, had a place in the Romantic Era. Sir Walter Scott published *Marmion,* which includes "Lochinvar," in 1808, and *The Bride of Triermain* in 1813. Both volumes deal with Arthurian figures. In 1816, two editions of Malory appeared. From this date, books relating to Arthuriana appear regularly until 1832, when Alfred Lord Tennyson published "The Palace of Art" and "The Lady of Shalott." He would continue his Arthurian writing until 1891, when he concluded the epilogue of *Idylls of the King.* The works of Scott and Tennyson profoundly influenced the popular culture of the period. Whereas Dickens dealt with the social ideals of the period, Tennyson translated its spiritual ideals. To the Victorian public such work offered a delightful alternative to the reality of the factory and the tediousness of the countinghouse.

The novels of Scott and the idylls of Tennyson found popularity in the United States as well as in England, suiting in particular the Cavalier Tradition of the South. In the mid-nineteenth century the agrarian South had the plantation and small farm as its basis. While a canal system connected the industrial Northwest with the Old Northwest, and the discovery of gold in California strengthened its ties to the financial community in the Northeast, the South, with its dependence upon England as a market for its tobacco and cotton, tended to become increasingly isolated. This, together with the Abolitionist Movement, helped to create a climate of opinion in which young Southerners saw themselves besieged in the defense of their way of life. They could identify with the Scottish Borderers and Highlanders depicted in the pages of Sir Walter Scott who were, in fact, the ancestors of the mountain people of the South.

The young men of the Confederacy, who valued horsemanship, ability with weapons and a sense of honor as well as style, traced these values back to their Cavalier Tradition, which in Virginia, Kentucky and Tennessee included the racing and breeding of horses and provided the cowboy of film and television with his most basic attribute. Gentlemen and farmers hunted, and ability with a gun became more valued as an attribute in the South than in the industrialized North. Thus, the *code duello,* dominant in New Orleans even after the Civil War, served as the basic model for the dramatic presentation of the gunfight.

The *Idylls of the King* suited the Cavalier Tradition and the South's young men went off to war armed with the sure and certain hope that they were knights defending their Camelot, the Confederacy. But the Confederacy fell, as had Camelot. Southerners were left with a dream and a ruined countryside. Many migrated West, as had others before the war, and they took their traditions and their memories with them. Prentiss Ingraham wrote of the adventures of Buffalo Bill and created Buck Taylor, King of the Cowboys, the first American pulp Western cowboy. Ingraham, raised and educated in the South and a fighter for the Confederacy, became responsible for the major influence exerted on pulp novels by the Arthurian tradition. One of his Buffalo Bill stories is even subtitled *The Knights of the Silver Circle.*[1]

The image of the knight becomes merged with that of the Western hero in the popular literature and the Western melodramas through the impress of writers like Ingraham who wrote cavalier tales, pirate stories and Westerns for the pulp-novel trade. These men also wrote the Western melodrama, which appeared on stages and in tents.

The trend accelerated when Westerners wore distinctive costumes, as did Wild Bill Hickok, Buffalo Bill Cody and General George Armstrong Custer. No doubt the publicity which accrued to men like Custer and Hickok encouraged the flamboyant style. Just as a knight could be distinguished by his colors and his coat of arms, Western heroes from Broncho Billy Anderson, Hopalong Cassidy, the Cisco Kid and "the man with no name" to Trinity can be identified by their costumes. Western actors like Tom Mix, Gene Autry and Roy Rogers also affected flamboyant costumes that would not seem out of place in a dime-novel melodrama. As with Ivanhoe and Lancelot, the costume of a Western character is often both an expression and a description of the character.

The central paradox of Tennyson's work, according to J. Phillip Eggers, lies in the "tension between human instincts and the ideals of civilization." [2] "The Lady of Shalott" embodies his concept of the aesthetic psyche "destroyed—like Camelot in the *Idylls*—in the clash between rules 'no man can keep' and her longing for the imperfect world of desire and Lancelot. . . . In all his Arthurian writings Tennyson stresses the conflict between spirit and sense and the harm man can cause Society and himself if he indulges in either sensual or spir-

---

[1] Ann Falk—personal communication.
[2] J. Philip Eggers, *King Arthur's Laureate.* New York: New York University Press, 1971, p. 6.

itual extremes."[3] The integration of Tennyson's Arthurian material into the Rationalist-Rousseauian structure of the American Western helped add a personal dimension to the historic clash between "Savagery and Civilization." The Arthurian influence contributes a characteristic style and a ready body of ideas and attitudes.

The immediate sources for the form and the action-oriented format associated with the Western film are the Western melodramas of the nineteenth century and Buffalo Bill's Wild West Show. The simple structure, the stress on fantastic action, the evil Indians, the rescue by the Cavalry and the hero capable of superhuman feats derive from stage melodramas. Robert Montgomery Bird's *Nick of the Woods* appeared as a novel in 1837. Louisa Medina Hamblin's adaptation was mounted in 1838 under the title of *The Jibbenainosay*, and productions continued until the 1860's and 70's. The play concerns a strange recluse who roamed the wilderness of Pennsylvania in Colonial days:[4]

He was sort of a Jekyll-Hyde character as border legend portrayed him. When it suited his purpose, he played the part of a misanthropic Quaker recluse [who] would never fight; and so well did he carry it off with his madman's cunning that none suspected him of being "bloody Nathan," a fleet and powerful killer who prowled along the border slaughtering every Indian who crossed his path and marking the carcasses with knife-slashes in the form of a cross on the breast. The tribes which suffered at his hands regard him with superstitious horror; to them he was "The Jibbenainosay," or walking spirit.[5]

A well-bred youth in his other life, Reginald Ashburn had watched his family and his bride scalped before his eyes by the Shawnee. He had since revenged himself upon all Red Men, regardless of tribe, while spending his life in search of the chief who had committed the outrage, Wenonga, "The Black Vulture of the Shawnees." The climax of the drama occurs when, at last, hunter and hunted clash in titanic combat.

The tradition of the "noble savage" stretches back to "L'Héroine Américaine" of Boulevard pantomine, and Major Robert Rogers' *Ponteach; or the Savages of America*, "the first American Indian play, never produced."[6] Cooper has Indians like Magua, the very personification of Evil, but he also relies upon Rousseau's "noble savage" as personified by Chingachgook.

[3] Eggers, p. 7.
[4] Frank Rahill, *The World of Melodrama*. University Park and London: Pennsylvania State University Press, 1967, p. 230.
[5] Rahill, p. 230.
[6] Rahill, p. 231.

What set *Nick of the Woods* apart from *Metamora,* which preceded it, and other dramas of the type and what entitles it to be considered the first authentically indigenous Wild West melodrama, is the absence from it of this "noble savage." [7]

The bad Indian replaced the convention of the "noble savage." He was joined in villainy by the Mexicans—the Mexicans taking the edge during the Mexican War. Later Anglo-Saxons and half-breed outlaws came to the fore.[8]

The melodrama *Nick of the Woods,* since it existed in a visual medium, contributed as much to the filmed Western as Cooper's "Leatherstocking Tales" contributed to the written Western. The stereotype of the bad, or lazy, drunken Indian became a more rigid stereotype in film than in the novel. Thrilling entrances such as Nick's "at the end of the second act where he precipitates down a cataract in a canoe of fire" [9] conform to the needs of the film maker. They go far to explain the emphasis on action that has dominated the Western since 1903. Audiences familiar with fast-moving Western melodramas knew what to expect when films began to move. Rather than filling a void, Westerns built on a dramatic tradition stretching back to 1838.

John Ford's classic film *The Searchers* (1956) bears more than a passing resemblance to *Nick of the Woods.* Ethan Edwards' (John Wayne's) mutilation of the dead warrior to keep him from seeing the way to the Happy Hunting Ground echoes Nick's bloody custom. Ethan pursues and ultimately kills in personal combat the chief who had led the massacre of his brother-in-law's family and kidnapped his niece. The family included the woman Ethan loved—his brother's wife—so, like Nick, Ethan avenges them. This contradictory figure, Ethan, who critics painfully attempt to explain away as a modern antihero tortured into the Western, made his debut in *Nick of the Woods.*

There is no one model for a Western hero as there is no one kind of true Western. The search for the true Western is a little like the search for the perfect woman, always doomed to frustration by the reality of human nature. The severe model which Nick provided was given swash and buckle by the addition of the Arthurian material. *Davy Crockett, or Be Sure You're Right, Then Go Ahead* by Frank Murdoch, revised extensively by the actor Frank Mayo, premiered in Rochester, New York, September 23, 1872. It remained a popular favorite until 1896 when Mayo, the leading actor, died.

Davy Crockett borrows its plot as well as its structure from Scott's

[7] Rahill, p. 231.
[8] Rahill, p. 232.
[9] Rahill, p. 231.

Young Lochinvar, as found in *Marmion*. Davy, unlike Deerslayer and Nick, functions as the Western hero and the romantic hero of the play. Attracted to Eleanor, the heroine, Davy hesitates because she is a lady, betrothed to someone of her own class, chosen by her guardian, and he only a backwoodsman. In Act II, Davy and Eleanor find themselves trapped by a snowstorm in a cabin, along with her fiancé, Neil, who is suffering with a fever. To pass the time, Eleanor reads Scott's "Lochinvar" to Davy. Davy's comments indicate that, though a rude frontierman, he possesses the natural nobility and sensitivity required of the romantic hero.

When Eleanor reads the sixth verse, which concludes:

> And the bride-maidens whisper'd, "Twere better by far
> To have match'd our fair cousin with your Lochinvar" [10]

Davy responds:

> True blue, and the gal's his—go it, you divil—oh, gal! Well, there's something in this rough breast of mine that leaps at the telling of a yarn like that. There's a fire—a smoldering fire that the breath of your voice has just kindled up into a blaze—a blaze that will sweep me down and leave my life a bed a ashes—of chilled and scattered ashes.[11]

After begging forgiveness for this untoward confession, Davy hears the wolves approach. The beasts hurl themselves against the door. Our hero must hold it closed with his own arm, having used the bar to fuel the fire. He proves himself worthy in deed as well as thought in that long night of holding the wolves at bay.

In true romantic tradition Davy doubts himself worthy to plight his troth, but like Lochinvar, his model, he arrives at Eleanor's home just in time to save her from forced marriage to a man she doesn't love. By doing so, Davy foils the villain's plot to gain control of her inheritance.

> One touch to her hand and one word in her ear,
> When they reached the hall-door, and the charger stood near;
> So light to the croupe the fair lady he swung,
> So light to the saddle before her he sprung!
> "She is won! we are gone, over bank, bush, and scaur;
> They'll have fleet steeds that follow", quoth young Lochinvar.

[10] Sir Walter Scott, *Marmion: A Tale of Flodden Field, in six cantos,* ed. by M. Macmillan. London: Macmillan & Co., 1887, p. 128.

[11] Frank Murdoch, *Davy Crockett, or Be Sure You're Right, Then Go Ahead,* in *Favorite Plays of the Nineteenth Century,* ed. by Barrett H. Clark. Princeton: Princeton University Press, 1943, p. 51.

There was racing and chasing on Cannobie Lee,
. . . But the lost bride of Netherby ne'er did they see.
So daring in love, and so dauntless in war,
Have ye e'er heard of gallant like young Lochinvar? [12]

In deference to pious sensibilities, Davy and Eleanor are married by
the parson, who just happens to drop in on Davy's mother. When her
guardian, his unscrupulous friend and her fiancé arrive, she and Davy
are already wed. The treatment of the Arthurian material indicates
that it represents a step forward in the development of the Western,
concerning itself not only with the simple problems of savagery vs.
civilization but also with the complex matters of class, money and romantic love. Davy rides a horse in the last act, in order to rescue Eleanor, although he is seen hunting on foot. The Cavalier Tradition in
the South is that of a horse culture. The use of material by Scott and
Tennyson helped insure that the hero of the filmed Western would be
a horseman, rather than a man afoot as were Nick of the Woods and
Natty Bumppo. Davy appears at a transitional period when the Arthurian material had been introduced, but had not yet been assimilated into the Western.

Buffalo Bill would embody the new Western hero. The year 1872
marked his debut as a stage performer, in Ned Buntline's melodrama
The Scouts of the Plains. This effort met with instant success, and the
play toured for two years. After 1882, Cody devoted himself to the
Buffalo Bill Wild West Show, the granddaddy of Republic Westerns.
Cowboys rode bucking horses, roped steers, rescued the Deadwood
stage from red Indians and thrilled most of the civilized world, Queen
Victoria included. In 1911 Thomas Ince hired Miller Brothers' 101
Wild West Show, which wintered in California. They appeared in the
Ince produced Westerns as well as those William S. Hart starred in
and directed for Ince. The flamboyance, the technical skill at riding,
roping and all-around stunt work associated with the Western film
stem from this intimate relationship with the Wild West Show.

Dime novels, Western melodramas and Wild West Shows were interrelated as the above paragraph indicates. Ned Buntline (Edward
Zane Carrel Judson) and Prentiss Ingraham wrote for the stage as well
as for the dime novel publishing house, Beadle and Adams. They
helped strengthen the cowboy's identification with the knight. The
effect of these, together with Ingraham's interest in Arthuriana, helped
shape the modern Western. Ingraham created the first "cowboy hero,"
Buck Taylor, in 1887. He fought with the Texas Rangers and wore
a diamond horseshoe on his hatband and as a tiepin. Buffalo Bill's
studied flamboyance and extravagantly costumed literary characters

[12] Scott, p. 128.

like Buck Taylor created a tradition into which Western stars like Tom Mix, Gene Autry and Roy Rogers fitted themselves. Audiences weaned on swashbuckling dime novels about pirates, outlaws, frontiermen and Wild West Shows knew what to expect when Mix rode on-screen astride Tony.

John Wayne's heroic persona seems reminiscent of Buffalo Bill. Like Buffalo Bill's, Wayne's dramatic persona merges with his person. On screen he is not just an actor essaying a role in a Western, he is a Western hero. As such, Wayne the actor could never do something of which Wayne the man did not approve. This tendency to blur the lines between actor and character would seem to originate in Buffalo Bill Cody's first timorous stage appearance in 1872.

Like modern Western heroes, Buffalo Bill appeared with a sidekick, his pal Texas Jack Omohundro. Actors like Walter Brennan, Gabby Hayes and Andy Devine who made their living from this kind of work probably have Texas Jack to thank. The well-known proclivity of sidekicks for bragging and even stretching the truth comes from a representative type who appears in the Wild West melodrama as early as *The Jibbenainosay* in the character of Roaring Ralph Stackpole, a rawboned, weatherbeaten frontierman afraid of nothing that walks or crawls and willing to tell the world about it. "He's a bellowing, rampageous roughneck and playboy, and even a hoss thief, though he insists that it is only Injun mounts he steals." [13] This "ring-tailed roarer" [14] thus had already become a standard character in farcical comedy by 1838. Victor McLaglen's portrayal of the brawling, boozing Sgt. Quincannon in *She Wore a Yellow Ribbon* (1949) and Victor Mature's interpretation of Doc Holliday in *My Darling Clementine* (1946) are reflections of his influence.

The brag of villain or sidekick tends to inflate the prowess of the speaker. The hero's brag communicates modest truth. Whenever Buffalo Bill shot, three Indians fell. The Drifter (Clint Eastwood) in *High Plains Drifter* (1973), when confronted by three toughs who threaten him, states: "I'm faster than you'll ever be," and shoots them dead when they draw. The villains have changed since Buffalo Bill rescued the maiden, but the prowess that enables the hero to save her remains the same. John Wayne demonstrated that when he rode down on the bad guys as Rooster Cogburn in *True Grit* (1969), two guns blazing and holding his reins in his teeth. Prentiss Ingraham would have loved to write such a scene.

Melodrama in the Bret Harte tradition exerted a more limited effect

[13] Rahill, p. 233.
[14] Stuart W. Hyde, "The Ring-Tailed Roarer in American Drama," *Southern Folklore Quarterly*, Vol. XIX, No. 3, September, 1955, pp. 171–78.

on Western film. Yet many critically acclaimed films fall within its boundaries. The stock characters—wastrels who sacrifice themselves for the waif-heroine, fancy women who become model wives, gamblers, comic Chinese cooks and rough miners with soft hearts[15]—will seem familiar to anyone who knows "Gunsmoke" and "Bonanza." In melodrama, "the Harte derivatives, . . . were excruciatingly emotional situations replacing in some degree the old-fashioned roughhouse and clowning; and these qualities tended to commend Western melodrama to audiences of more fastidious taste." [16] This school was exemplified by works such as Frank Hitchcock Murdoch's *Davy Crockett* (1872) and David Belasco's *Girl of the Golden West* (1905). "Virtually every writer of gold rush plays from the seventies onward used the stock Harte character types" [17] and his patented brand of sentimentality.

Broncho Billy Anderson followed Harte's conventions in his movies. He established the version of the convention with which moviegoers became familiar in *Broncho Billy and the Baby,* an adaptation of Peter Kyne's story about an outlaw who reforms when he elects to save a sick child rather than escape the posse. William S. Hart subscribes to this convention in *The Disciple,* in which he plays a missionary. An oily gambler, "Doc" Hardy (Holliday), has lured away the missionary's wife. In typical Bret Harte fashion, the wife returns, in the middle of a blizzard, when her child is ill. The gambler cures the child, the family reunites and the father returns to his missionary work. Harte's theme of the wastrel sacrificing himself for the waif-heroine tends, in films, to transform into that of the gunman who sacrifices himself, or at least sacrifices, for a baby or child. *Shane* (1953) reflects this convention in the relationship between Shane (Alan Ladd) and Joey (Brandon DeWilde). *Three Godfathers* (1948) and its predecessor *Marked Men* (1919), both by John Ford, employ the convention as three bank robbers struggle across a desert with a baby. So that the child may live, two of the outlaws die and the third, played by John Wayne, gives up his freedom.

The influence of the two schools of Western melodrama, the dime-novel school and the Bret Harte school, affects all Westerns and it would be a dubious exercise to separate out Westerns reflecting one school or the other. Each has contributed necessary elements. The flamboyance is as inherent to the tradition as is the hooker with the heart of gold.

The dime-novel and Bret Harte schools of Western melodrama, and the influence of the Arthurian tradition, all brought their influence

[15] Rahill, p. 237.
[16] Rahill, p. 237.
[17] Rahill, p. 237.

to bear on the development of Western film. Early film makers like William S. Hart were associated with theater and carried the realism then in vogue to its logical extreme with film. While the techniques of staging and stagecraft made popular by Henry Irving and David Belasco could be transferred to the screen intact with logical improvement, a director like John Ford would build upon the popular theater and literature of his youth throughout his career.

Cultural Origins of the Western
by RICHARD W. ETULAIN

In the first quarter of the present century, a new American cultural type—the Western—arose. Because until recently historians and students of literature have paid scant attention to popular culture, the Western has received little notice. Those who have chosen to discuss this popular genre have usually dismissed it as trash or as a species of subculture.[1] This being the case, no one has undertaken a study of the origins of the Western. This paper is a very brief and tentative treatment of the rise of the Western and why it arose when it did.

Some students of popular culture contend that the roots of the Western can be traced back to Homer and other writers of the epic. Others suggest that it owes most of its ingredients to medieval romances and morality plays. And still others argue that Sir Walter Scott, Robert Louis Stevenson, and other writers of historical adventure influenced the shape and content of the Western more than any other source. Each of these arguments has its validity, but the major reasons for the rise of the Western are found in more recent trends in American cultural history. More than anything else the genre owes its appearance to the combined influence of a number of occurrences in the years surrounding 1900. Each of these events or changes may have been largely independent of the rest, but all shared in giving rise to an indigenous cultural type.[2]

From Journal of Popular Culture, V (Spring 1972), 799–805. This essay appeared therein in slightly different form as "Origins of the Western." Reprinted by permission of the author and Bowling Green Popular Press.

[1] For an example of this negative attitude: "It has been the fate of the American West to beget stereotypes that belong to pseudo art before it has yielded up the individual types that belong to art proper." Robert B. Heilman, "The Western Theme: Exploiters and Explorers." Partisan Review, XXVIII (March–April 1961), 286.

[2] Especially helpful for the remarks in this paragraph and in the paragraphs that follow are Henry Nash Smith, Virgin Land: The American West as Symbol and Myth. New York: Vintage Books, 1957, pp. 88–137; E. Douglas Branch, The Cowboy and His Interpreters. New York: Cooper Square Publishers, 1960, pp. 180–270; Joe

The appearance of a new hero in American literature—the cowboy—offered distinctive experiences for the author of the Western to
portray. As Warren French and Mody Boatright have pointed out, the
cowboy appeared earlier in a few dime novels but nearly always as a
minor figure and frequently in an ungallant role. By 1890, however,
the cowboy was beginning to move to the forefront as a Western fictional hero. Commencing with the writings of Owen Wister he received a new emphasis. This newly refurbished hero aided greatly the
rise of the Western.[3]

Also, about 1900 there was a revival of interest in the historical
novel—one of three such periods in American literary history. Americans turned to historical fiction as one possible formula for recapturing a past that they were reluctant to lose. Because the Western was
historical or pseudohistorical, it benefited from the revival of interest
in the historical novel.[4]

Moreover, there was an increased interest in the West during the
last two decades of the nineteenth century. A series of critical economic problems brought to mind a sobering truth: the West was filling up; its wide-open spaces might soon vanish. Tourists flocked west,
and a number published their reactions to the region in such influential eastern magazines as *Outlook, Harper's, Scribner's,* and *At-
lantic.* These same periodicals took more western fiction in the 1880's,
and the western pieces became so popular by the middle 1890's that
Henry Alden, an editor of *Harper's Monthly,* did his best to keep all
of Owen Wister's work in his magazine. Several editors wanted Wister's fiction, and only higher prices kept him in the *Harper's* fold.[5]

The era from 1890 to 1910 has frequently been termed "the strenu-
ous age." The fiction of Jack London, Harold Bell Wright, Stewart
Edward White, Rex Beach, and other writings of the rough, virile,

---

B. Frantz and Julian E. Choate, *The American Cowboy: Myth and Reality.* London:
Thames and Hudson, 1956, pp. 140–79; G. Edward White, *The Eastern Establish-
ment and the Western Experience: The West of Frederic Remington, Theodore
Roosevelt, and Owen Wister.* New Haven: Yale University Press, 1968, especially
pp. 31–51; and Russel B. Nye, *The Unembarrassed Muse: The Popular Arts in
America.* New York: Dial Press, 1970, pp. 280–304.

[3] Warren French, "The Cowboy in the Dime Novel." *Texas Studies in English,*
XXX (1951), 219–34; Mody C. Boatright, "The Beginning of Cowboy Fiction."
Southwest Review, LI (Winter 1966), 11–28.

[4] Willard Thorp, *American Writing in the Twentieth Century.* Cambridge: Har-
vard University Press, 1960, pp. 1–11; Ernest E. Leisy, *The American Historical
Novel.* Norman: University of Oklahoma Press, 1950, pp. 9–17.

[5] Earl Pomeroy, *In Search of the Golden West: The Tourist in Western America.*
New York: Alfred A. Knopf, 1957, pp. 73–111; L. J. Shaul, "Treatment of the West
in Selected Magazine Fiction, 1870–1910—An Annotated Bibliography." Unpublished
master's thesis, University of Wyoming, 1954, pp. 50–52. The Alden-Wister relationship and other details about readers' interests in western fiction published during
the 1890's is exhibited in the Owen Wister Papers, Library of Congress.

and out-of-doors type speak for the age. It was the period of the Span-
ish-American War generation, of Teddy Roosevelt, of militant Anglo-
Saxonism. This spirit is found in the Western, particularly in its
portrayal of the gallant hero who is always eager to combat any foe,
regardless of the odds.

By the early 1890's interest in the dime novel was diminishing.
Shortly after its inception during the Civil War, this popular type had
turned to the West for several of its heroes—Buffalo Bill, Deadwood
Dick, Old Scout, and other frontier worthies. As the dime novel began to disappear, the popularity of its hero fell rapidly. Readers undoubtedly were dissatisfied with a continuous line of heroes who
fought off twenty Indians and rescued the heroine, even with one arm
badly wounded. They wanted a gallant and strong protagonist but
one that was, nonetheless, believable. Eventually, the hero of the
Western satisfied both of these desires.[6]

The Western also continued an American melodramatic tradition
that had appeared earlier in such sources as the writings of James
Fenimore Cooper, the dime novel, and the works of the sentimental
novelists. In the post-Civil War period western literature became a
recognizable current in the stream of melodrama. The work of Bret
Harte, the dime novelists, and the story-paper writers firmly established the melodramatic tradition in the literature of the West. As one
study of the western periodical literature of the late nineteenth century points out, western writers increasingly utilized vague western
settings and general descriptions. And a nostalgic tone crept into
western literature. It was as if those who had lived through the previous years were, by 1890 and afterward, looking back and trying to
recapture some of their past glory.[7]

Finally, the most important reason for the rise of the Western is
the most difficult to describe with precision. This factor is what historian Carl Becker calls the "climate of opinion" of an era. In this
case, it is the predominant mentality of the Progressive period in
American history.

Several interpreters have described the Progressive Era as a water-
shed period in the American mind. From the 1890's until World War
I a new urban, industrial thrust in American society challenged the
older mentality of a rural, agricultural America. For Americans who
became Progressives, or who shared the moods and feelings of the
Progressives, this conflict between the old and the new was a trau-
matic experience that was not easily resolved.

[6] Wallace Stegner, "Western Record and Romance," *Literary History of the United
States,* ed. Robert Spiller and others. New York: The Macmillan Company, 1960,
pp. 862–64, 872.
[7] Smith, *Virgin Land,* pp. 88–137; Mary Noel, *Villains Galore.* New York: The
Macmillan Company, 1954, pp. 131–32, 149–59; Shaul, "Treatment of the West,"
pp. 51–52.

Many Progressives were forward-looking. Like Theodore Roosevelt, they accepted the new urban-industrial force and advocated a federal government strong enough to deal with the powerful energies that the cities and industrial capitalists had unleashed. The New Nationalists, as they were called, were optimistic reformers and called for strong, new leadership to deal with current problems.

Another strain of the Progressive mind that owed much to Populism is evident in the early ideas of Woodrow Wilson. He too thought that the rise of an urban-industrial America necessitated changes in the forms of government and society. But Wilson and his followers thought the necessary reform was that of breaking up large corporations and of returning to a pre-industrial America, of recapturing Jefferson's agrarian dream. If these advocates of New Freedom allowed themselves to do so, they easily slipped into a nostalgic longing for pre-Rockefeller, Carnegie, and Vanderbilt days.

The same nostalgia that was apparent among proponents of New Freedom was also evident among followers of New Nationalism. In several ways Roosevelt stands as a Janus figure: the venturesome technocrat and yet the advocate of individualism, the product of an eastern-Harvard gentility and yet the westerner and Rough Rider. Other Americans of the era shared Roosevelt's feelings: the desire to hold on to the fruits of industrialism without losing, at the same time, individual freedom. For these persons, the American West was the last frontier of freedom and individualism, and it had to be preserved as a sacred bulwark against profane industrialism.

And thus the West as a physical and spiritual frontier was an important symbol for Americans during the Progressive Era. To lose it or the idyllic existence that it represented was to lose part of their past and to bargain away their future. It is not difficult to perceive how this psychological necessity encouraged authors to devote more attention to the West in their writings. The need and mood were apparent, and writers who were a part of this identity crisis—or at least sensed it—could assure themselves a larger audience if they portrayed the West romantically. So the conflict between industrial and agricultural America and the resultant nostalgia for the past were large encouragements for the rise of the Western.[8]

[8] More recently, this relationship is dealt with in White's *The Eastern Establishment and the Western Experience*; and in David Noble's several books on the Progressives, particularly in his latest book, *The Progressive Mind, 1890–1917*. Chicago: Rand McNally, 1970. Peter Schmitt adds another dimension in his stimulating monograph *Back to Nature: The Arcadian Myth in Urban America*. New York: Oxford University Press, 1969. Finally, Roderick Nash and John William Ward suggest that the clash between past and present was a pivotal tension in the twenties. See Nash's *The Nervous Generation: American Thought, 1917–1930*. Chicago: Rand McNally, 1970, and Ward's "The Meaning of Lindbergh's Flight." *American Quarterly*, X (Spring 1958), 3–16.

These trends were John the Baptists in preparing the way for the fictional Western. Such writers as Owen Wister, Zane Grey, and Frederick Faust (Max Brand), sometimes working within the limits of these trends and sometimes pressured into new directions by them, did much to establish the dimensions of the Western. Wister, for example, utilized the new cowboy hero and the Wyoming past and blended them with the necessary ingredients of adventure fiction—love, action, and good versus evil—to produce the first Western in *The Virginian* (1902). He was, in short, the synthesizer of the elements that make up the Western. Following the pattern that Wister introduced, Grey and Brand, though men of lesser writing talents, turned out dozens of Westerns by the end of the 1920's.

These cultural strains mentioned above—what John Higham has called the "reorientation of American culture in the 1890's"—also helped shape the first Western movies. Early experiments with western scenes and figures began even before the turn of the century, although most film historians cite Edwin S. Porter's *The Great Train Robbery* (1903) as perhaps the first film Western. By 1910 the genre was sufficiently established that critics began to deal with it as a separate type.[9]

Like its fictional sidekick, the Western film drew upon the strong contemporary interest in things western. The Wild West Shows of Buffalo Bill Cody were particularly important in paving the way for the entrance of the Western movies. Many of the scenes from these shows could be and were duplicated on the early screen. And directors soon capitalized upon the cowboy as their leading male hero. Portraying the man on horseback as something of an "adult Boy Scout," they immediately made the cowpoke into a type hero. G. M. Anderson, later known on screen as 'Broncho Billy,'' realized the need for a popular hero, and he more than anyone else decided to center on the cowboy as *the* star of the Western. Anderson made nearly four hundred short Westerns; he was the Max Brand of the Western film industry.

Directors accented the epic theme of westering. Even in the first film Westerns, the outdoors was an important ingredient. Gradually more emphasis was placed on the westward movement as *the* theme of our history; by stressing the pioneers' struggle with and settling of the West, movie-makers helped fulfill vicarious psychological needs of the time. Later, producers made increasing use of the western scene,

[9] John Higham, "The Reorientation of American Culture in the 1890's," in *The Origins of Modern Consciousness*, ed. John Weiss. Detroit: Wayne State University Press, 1965, pp. 25–48. For my comments on the Western film I have relied most heavily on George N. Fenin and William K. Everson, *The Western: From Silents to Cinerama*. Bonanza Books: New York, 1962.

and audiences were eventually treated to grandiose perspectives like those seen in John Ford's *Stagecoach* of the 1930's.

In several ways, *The Great Train Robbery* holds a position in the development of the Western film similar to that of *The Virginian* in the rise of the fictional Western. The movie capitalized on American interest in such western worthies as Butch Cassidy and the Wild Bunch boys and utilized tales of their adventures to add zest to the film. Porter's movie emphasized some of the same elements as Wister's novel: chase and pursuit, the outdoors, and gunfights between heroes and villains. And, above all, as one account has put it, Porter's film should be seen "not so much as a Western, but as a *blueprint* for *all* Westerns." The same could be said about *The Virginian*.

The roots of the Western, then, were nourished by cultural and intellectual currents that rippled through American experience between the end of the nineteenth century and the Depression. Roderick Nash, who examines this era's need for wilderness symbols, expresses as well as anyone the cultural-intellectual matrix that helped spawn the Western. He says:

America was ripe for the widespread appeal of the uncivilized. The cult had several facets. In the first place, there was a growing tendency to associate wilderness with America's frontier and pioneer past that was believed responsible for many unique and desirable national characteristics. Wilderness also acquired importance as a source or virility, toughness, and savagery—qualities that defined fitness in Darwinian terms. Finally, an increasing number of Americans invested wild places with aesthetic and ethical values, emphasizing the opportunity they afforded for contemplation and worship.[10]

What Nash points out—and this is a point that students of American popular culture must keep in mind—is that the origins of a new popular idea or genre are usually tied to specific occurrences in the mind and experience of the era that produces them. So it was with the beginnings of the Western.

[10] Roderick Nash, *Wilderness and the American Mind*. New Haven: Yale University Press, 1967, p. 145.

S. Porter was a technician and a mechanic rather than a re-
and creative film maker. But his one-reel *The Great Train*
(Edison, 1903) was the first narrative Western and it estab-
e basic cinematic pattern for subsequent Western production:
ursuit, retribution. *The Train Robbers* (Warner's, 1972) dif-
 in that it ends before the retribution is quite finished.
ugh he may never have been on a horse before, G. M. Ander-
 had been hired by Porter, managed to play four roles in the
 was impressed by the financial prospects of the Western, es-
in view of the continuing box-office success of *The Great Train*
y. By 1908 Anderson was in partnership with George K. Spoor
ago and their Essanay company was in the process of producing
of one-reel Westerns to be shot on location. Anderson was the
do this. Eventually others followed suit. California, it seemed
erson, offered the best climate. As the 'Teens began, most of
stern companies were sending troupes to the West Coast or
g studios there expressly to film outdoor dramas.
rson's influence on the screen treatment of the West is surely
al of any of the technical innovations employed by D. W. Grif-
 was Anderson's conviction that a Western must have a central
er. In 1909 he purchased for fifty dollars the screen rights to the
er "Broncho Billy," which Peter B. Kyne had featured in a
e wrote for *The Saturday Evening Post*. Anderson's first star-
Vestern, *The Bandit Makes Good* (Essanay, 1908), was not a
lm. The character made its debut in 1910 in the film *Broncho*
Redemption. Anderson's favorite role was that of a good bad
The name became a moniker and Anderson played the same
ter in all of his subsequent films until he left Essanay in 1915.
son later concluded that during the years 1908–15 he had pro-
 concluded that during the years 1908–15 he had pro-
 and appeared in some 375 short Westerns. Few of these sur-
although more are in the British Film Institute than at the Li-
of Congress and other American archives. Fortunately two of
hest films, made at the twilight of his career, *Shootin' Mad*, a
eler of 1918, and *The Son-of-a-Gun*, his last Western and only
e-length picture, can still be seen.
derson constantly strove to improve the production values of hi
res and so his last are his best. But in content he stayed er
hed in the traditional melodrama typical of the pulps of h
I think we are inclined to forget today the degree of snobber
which films were met in the beginning. The pay was good b
ocial esteem made seeking work in them a last-ditch compromis

The American Western Cinema: 1903–Present
by JON TUSKA

I

The Red Pony was remade as a motion picture for television and broadcast over NBC on 18 March 1973. You may or may not care for the John Steinbeck short novel. But he gives his character of the Grandfather a brilliant soliloquy. Grandfather once led a wagon train west. He tells twelve-year-old Jody, his grandson, about his adventures. According to the screenplay based on Steinbeck's dialogue, when Jody suggests that maybe someday he could be a leader of the people, Grandfather shakes his head no. "There's no place to go, son. There's the ocean to stop you. Every place is taken. It's all done now. Westering is finished."

It is difficult, if not impossible, to draw theoretical conclusions about the significance of the Western cinema when so little that is accurate has been written about its history. Nor have most critics seen what remains of the films spanning seven decades. I believe in being thorough. I have screened more than eight thousand Westerns. I would not recommend that anyone else do it. There has been no appreciable change in my personality or temperament as a consequence. My moral convictions—or utter lack of them—remain unassailed. But you cannot undergo an experience of this kind and not come away with some impressions.

I cannot pretend in this essay to clear up the countless fantasies and delusions which have come to be accepted as facts about Western production and personnel. But there are a few observations I would like to pass on to the reader as to how one best approaches a motion picture and in particular a Western as an object of critical study rather

From Views and Reviews (*February 1974*). *Reprinted by permission of the author.*

25

than as an entertainment. The truth of film is emotional truth. When you get right down to it successful pictures, like successful stories, are about individual people. Whatever the location, or the historical setting, or the great events used as a backdrop—and these may be very important to the film as a composite—it's the people in it that matter, and the action that centers around them. The traditional Western has reinforced American individualism.

John Ford has won four Academy Awards for direction and recently has become the topic of academic interest. Many critics have complained that he refuses to answer their questions directly or, at times, even intelligently. They expect him to be analytical about his films. He can't. He didn't make them that way. His films are about the characters in them. All of the bits of business he has invented off the cuff, or the spontaneous dialogue he has achieved by emending the printed script, have been attempts to amplify peculiarities of personality. A good director intuitively *feels* these things. They are planned; they have an instinctive rightness. But they are the result of a creative synthesis, not analysis.

A film is a collective and necessarily corporate enterprise. Every person working on a picture contributes his share to its effectiveness. When one man fails, you can spot his blunder more readily than you ever can see the working parts when everyone does his best and the illusion of the film is uniformly sustained.

Motion pictures are produced in order to make money. It is successful cinema—does business at the box office—when the story told fills the public's emotional needs in such a way as to induce them to pay hard cash for the experience of it. Grosses cannot determine artistic quality or technical achievement, but grosses are a reflection of popular sentiment. And popular sentiment is a film maker's stock in trade. A film may occasionally be a personal expression. So long as the personal expression parallels popular sentiment, the financial results will be favorable. When popular sentiment changes, so must a film maker's orientation, or he is done.

The Western since 1903 has been a safer bet withal than any other kind of picture. Americans prefer it among genre films. What the French or the Egyptians may think of Westerns isn't important to our filmmakers—not because of any narrow chauvinistic bias but simply because, to this day, for foreign and domestic films alike the United States is still *the* primary market. Economic conditions prior to World War II were such that the foreign market alone could maintain Greta Garbo as a star. No more. Films may be produced abroad but, usually, they cannot be financially successful without the American theater-going public.

Were you to talk to men like Colonel Tim McCoy or John Ford,

Anderson was an unsuccessful stage actor. D. W. Griffith was a fizzle as a playwright. Bill Hart did not have an illustrious time of it before the footlights, nor did Francis Ford, who became a serial hero. When these men came to make movies, they brought with them all the heavy sentimentality of the American legitimate theater of the previous century. The cynicism following the Great War altered public sentiment and brought much of this excessive sentimentalism to an end. John Ford, Francis' younger brother, was one of the few survivors.

Probably the single most important figure in the history of the silent Western is a man no one appears to be aware of any longer. It was his character and temperament that shaped and influenced nearly all Western production in Hollywood from 1915–35. The Fords worked for him. Jack Holt starred in the first Western serial for him. Thomas Ince got his start with him. At one time or another Harry Carey, Hoot Gibson, Art Acord, Roy Stewart, Tim McCoy, Ken Maynard, Buck Jones and Tom Mix all worked on his lot and in nearly every case produced their most memorable films on his generous budgets. This was because no man in the motion picture industry loved Westerns as much as emigrant, five-foot, beaming Uncle Carl Laemmle, the Little Champ, president of Universal Film Manufacturing Co.

Uncle Carl had arrived in the New World penniless, unfamiliar with the language or customs. But he had daring, perseverance, guts and charisma. He battled against the Film Patents Trust and won. He hired Edwin S. Porter on the basis of *The Great Train Robbery*. When he opened Universal City in 1915, he introduced the assembly-line concept to film production. He gathered stock companies of players.

Laemmle signed Harry Carey to make a series of Westerns to compete with the Billy films just as Anderson was leaving Essanay. John Ford cut his teeth as a director on the Carey pictures. Hoot Gibson got his chance with Carey, first as a double, then working into lead roles. The format of the Carey Westerns was soon changed from two-reelers to features. John Ford's first feature survives, *Straight Shooting* (Universal, 1917). It is by no means a great Western. Ford savants see in it techniques Ford supposedly learned while playing a Klansman in *The Birth of a Nation* (Epoch, 1915). I find this sort of speculation preposterous. We have an insufficient number of silent films from the 'Teens intact—much less easily accessible to viewing by these critics —to be able to say anything very intelligent about who borrowed what from whom. It makes good copy, but it has no historical foundation.

Whatever his pardonable failings, Uncle Carl (called that because of the number of Old Country relatives he employed) loved cowboys and Western films. He gave his directors a splendid freedom. By the mid-twenties, actors like Hoot Gibson, and later Ken Maynard, Tom Mix and Buck Jones, had incorporated their own units and were directly responsible for the production of their Westerns. Universal financed and had only general story approval. Gibson's films from 1925–30, Maynard's from 1929–30 and 1933–34, Mix's in 1932–33 and Jones' from 1934–37 were extremely personal vehicles and were made the way they intended them to be made. No series Westerns subsequently made by any studio show the individual stamp and distinct personality of the lead players as do these Universal entries. Right or wrong, Uncle Carl felt that cowboys knew most about how Westerns should be made.

Nearly the whole of Universal's silent library is unavailable. In the mid-Fifties, when MCA had assumed control of the company, the executives had to decide whether to finance transfer from nitrate to acetate stock or destroy all prints and negatives. After much deliberation, the latter course was chosen. I believe it was economically sound as a business decision; in terms of historical assessment and study, it remains a tragedy. The sound Westerns of Gibson, Maynard, Mix and Jones, most of which have been saved by MCA, deserve very serious attention and I will come back to them.

The assembly-line concept of Western production had wide influence. Universal and the independent companies in the Twenties specialized in producing "B," or budget, Westerns as well as, in Universal's case, specials, or "A" feature Westerns. In the Forties and Fifties, John Ford persisted in the stock company concept; Duke Wayne relies on a stock company to the present day. Universal maintained its "B" line of Westerns and serials until 1946, when it shut down all units; other firms continued the practice theatrically until 1954 and then applied it to television production. Universal City Studios, which depends heavily on television markets currently, has simply refined concepts which Uncle Carl borrowed from Detroit automobile manufacturers in 1915.

III

D. W. Griffith, whom Porter hired at the Edison company, left and began directing one- and two-reelers for Biograph in 1908. By subsequent standards, he had a chaotic way of working. He avoided scripts. No one, including Griffith, could foretell what a film would look like until it was edited. In a time of unlimited enthusiasm, guaranteed box office and a general air of improvisation, Griffith made a staggering number of "bombs"—this is the *technical* term for failure in the industry—but when everything coalesced, whipped into a frenzy by D. W.'s passionate zeal, he raised the art of the silent film above the need for spoken language.

In 1910, Griffith took his company to California. He was dissatisfied with New Jersey locations for his Westerns. He borrowed his horses from a group of wranglers, among them Hoot Gibson, who did occasional stunt work and appeared on camera as Henry B. Walthall's double in *Two Brothers* (Biograph, 1910). Carey began his career in films working for Griffith in the same year. Walthall, Gibson and Carey would appear together in the final important Western for all of them, *The Last Outlaw* (RKO, 1936), based on a John Ford screenplay from Carey's Cheyenne Harry-Universal days.

There's been much debate over whether or not Lionel Barrymore appeared in D. W.'s *Fighting Blood* (Biograph, 1911). I've seen it forty times and I can't tell you. What *is* significant about this film is Griffith's staging of an Indian attack on a blockhouse and a rescue by the cavalry. What he learned from this one-reeler he applied ingeniously in *The Battle At Elderbush Gulch* (Biograph, 1913), among surviving materials unquestionably Griffith's finest Western.

Technically both *Elderbush Gulch* and *The Birth of a Nation,* if they didn't innovate, at least incorporated a number of devices which became staples in Western production. Both build up to climaxes in which seemingly doomed characters are saved at the last minute from certain death. The editing of the ride of the Klan to create breathtaking suspense was utilized in many Westerns henceforth and especially in Hoot Gibson Specials during the Twenties. One of the Midwest franchisees of *Birth* was Harry "Pop" Sherman, who became a Western film maker himself in the Thirties, first with the Bar 20 series based on Clarence E. Mulford's novels about Hopalong Cassidy and numerous other characters, and then as producer of the last entries in the Paramount Zane Grey series plus several "A" Westerns later for United Artists release. "Pop" admitted his indebtedness to Griffith. He once summed up his successful formula for Westerns as "Open big, forget the middle and come to a terrific finish." It worked. "Pop" personally made some fifteen million dollars using that one idea.

William S. Hart, for all the prestige he now enjoys, was an anomaly. When he came to pictures he was forty-four years old. Thomas Ince, for whom he worked, did *not* discover him nor did he even want Hart to star in a Western. However, after much deliberation Ince did contract Hart and backed his films for theatrical release. Hart was a better actor than G. M. Anderson and his portrayals had greater depth. He caught on rapidly with the public and as the 'Teens closed ranked prominently at the box office among Western players.

I call Hart an anomaly because, while he did have a distinctive and individual screen style, his influence on Western film making was negligible. I said before that very few Westerns from the 'Teens survive. No one can depend on anything but memory and the trades to tell you what Tom Mix's early Fox Westerns from 1917–19 looked like. When Hart made his first feature, *The Bargain* (N. Y. M. P. C., 1914), his only real competition came from the Anderson two-reelers and they were nearly at an end. You'll find the same crudity of dress, dilapidated town sets, dusty streets, rough interiors—the "realism" praised in the Hart Westerns—in Anderson's pictures of that period and in Universal products like *Straight Shooting* or the Selig short Westerns with Tom Mix. Since most of Hart's Westerns still exist, in lieu of any ready contradiction he is given credit for introducing these elements. To me this appears more the consequence of hindsight come of the absurd gaudiness of the musical Westerns that began in the mid-Thirties and, earlier, the glamor introduced by the Ken Maynard virtuoso vehicles commencing in 1926 with First National's *Senor Daredevil*. Contrast with these later Westerns makes the Hart films a novel, even startling experience. Had we more documentation by means of which to trace stylistic evolution, I suggest it might turn out that Westerns were so "realistic" in the 'Teens because film makers couldn't imagine them being any other way. They were still too near the Old West to dare conceive films as brazenly absurd as the Autry fantasies of the sound era.

Ince had not made a starring Western series before Hart's. He thought little of Bill Hart as a person at the beginning of their association and he took minimal interest in the production of the Hart films for the duration of Hart's contract. The fortune Triangle amassed from the Hart Westerns was wasted on films with New York stage players that died at the box office. Unlike Carl Laemmle, Ince cared nothing about Westerns, regarding them as a necessary, if slightly embarrassing, commodity the revenues from which could be used to finance more ambitious artistic projects.

Ince permitted Hart relatively generous budgets for the time. The features cost between $13–15,000 and went at least a month in production. This figure is amusing to compare with $125,000 budgets at Paramount in the Twenties for their first Zane Grey Westerns, the $500,000 at Universal for Hoot Gibson's *The Calgary Stampede* in 1926 and Sam Katzman's $8,000 budgets for Tim McCoy *sound* Westerns in 1938–39, with McCoy getting $4,000 of the $8,000 as salary and filming the productions in two days and a night!

Curiously, those critics who prefer Hart's Westerns tend to favor his early work at Triangle as opposed to his later films for Paramount on $150,000 budgets. Ince initially gave Hart a good crew, with Reginald Barker directing and C. Gardner Sullivan doing the scenarios. In 1915, Hart directed a series of short Westerns and began to develop his concepts of Western film making, moving on in October, 1915, to the feature *The Disciple,* and following with *Hell's Hinges* in 1916. Hart's subsequent career in Hollywood proved that, whatever else he was, he was no director.

If you divorce these Westerns from their physical austerity and the raw reproduction of the panchromatic film stock on which they were photographed, Hart's pictures are unique, but in a somewhat unexpected fashion. Hart's plots as plots are *not* realistic. They are keenly romantic, sentimental, melodramatic, occasionally ridiculous—but ridiculous in the spirit of Don Quixote. You do not doubt for a moment the knightly sincerity with which Hart undergoes his religious conversions or emotes in the throes of a throbbing self-recrimination. Not until his last film, *Tumbleweeds,* in 1925, did Hart alleviate this heavy emotional atmosphere with less oppressive moments of bright comedy. Hart was obsessed with his personal conception of the West and his vision of its heroes—gripped in the same frantic thralldom in which Clarence E. Mulford, in his home at Bridgeport, Connecticut, dreamed of a solitary meal on the prairie, a noisy cattle town or tinkered with the small pieces of wood from his facsimile of the Alamo. History and romance were inseparable, even beautiful to them as they sometimes are for essentially lonely men.

For my taste I would choose Hart's Paramount titles, *Wagon Tracks* (1919) and *The Toll Gate* (1920)—and, of course, above all, *Tumbleweeds. Wagon Tracks* had nowhere near the astonishing response of *The Covered Wagon* (Paramount, 1923), but it was frankly a better film. Hart steeped himself in the lore of the West. More important than his "realism" or his romanticism was his factuality. His comment on seeing *The Covered Wagon* was that no responsible wagon master would camp his train in a box canyon. His observation on the stage race across the salt flats in *Stagecoach* (United Artists, 1939) was that an intelligent Indian would have shot one of the horses and ended the race. He knew what he was doing factually and *Wagon Tracks,* splendidly photographed by Joseph August and directed by Lambert Hillyer and Hart, wove a spell of poetic grandeur about a long trek westward through Indian lands. It has a documentary character in its attention to detail.

The probable reason Cruze's *Covered Wagon* and *Stagecoach* did so well, even with their discrepancies, consists in this: you can readily respond to and identify with the actions and feelings of the persons in the respective stories. The characters are cinematic and true to life. What ruined Hart in actually a very short time was his dogged insistence on overstated, fragrant, idealistic and sentimental plots. Hart overplays all his scenes. He *feels* too much. He doesn't let the audience feel. If the screenplay calls for an emotional close-up of Hart's face, there is no ambiguity; the tears stand in his eyes. When, for example, in *Rio Grande* (Republic, 1950) John Ford wanted a close-up of Duke

Wayne, he instructed Duke to show nothing and *think* of nothing. Let the audience project the misery and determination accented by the harsh lighting with the silver, moonlit water of the great river casting a pale hue upon haggard features. The emotion arose in the audience —where it was supposed to be—not on the screen. For all of his many virtues, William S. Hart was not a consummate film maker. He never learned how to thrill audiences at the same time as he might impress them.

IV

By the Twenties the star system was solidly entrenched. The plots mattered less than *who* appeared in them. Tom Mix had the largest public following.

Sol Wurtzel was in charge of the Fox West Coast studio. He let the Mix unit make their Westerns as it suited them. Mix himself was a flamboyant, fun-loving personality who stressed excitement, stunting and cavalier bravado in his films. His cinematographer, Daniel Clark, was one of the best in the business. Clark as much as Mix helped create the superhuman qualities in Mix's heroes through subtle camera setups and flattering oppositions. Mix sought out unusual locations and national park sites for many of his Westerns. When John Ford joined Fox, he directed several Mix pictures.

William S. Hart had made his horse, Fritz, into nearly a co-star although he temporarily "retired" him until his contract with Ince expired. Mix latched on to this idea and used Old Blue and then Tony in a similar manner. Mix had a theatrical streak that other Westerners didn't—in such flagrant abundance. Tony wasn't merely a friend; he dazzled audiences with amazing equestrian feats. But it wasn't all for the camera. Ken Maynard loved Tarzan as he never did a human being. When Buck Jones died, Silver stopped eating and succumbed soon after. It is almost ludicrous that Hart's impact on later Westerns should have come to this.

Not many of Mix's feature Westerns from the Twenties survive, and some that do, like *Just Tony* (Fox, 1922), are not readily available. *Sky High* (Fox, 1922) has some precarious footage with Mix engaging in stunts on the rim and along the narrow trails of the Grand Canyon. *The Great K & A Train Robbery* (Fox, 1927) employed a railroad setting, always a Mix favorite, with a story that moved and was filled with humor and action.

Mix made repeated importunities for more money, so that by 1919 he was earning ten thousand dollars a week and more than that if the money he received for his personal appearances is counted in. He then went on strike for seventeen thousand dollars a week. His pictures were supporting the studio and he felt well within his rights. Buck Jones, who was working for Fox as a double and had had minimum exposure in a few Franklyn Farnum independent two-reelers, was then offered a contract. Winifred Sheehan wrote to him on 9 October 1919, advising him on his vice-presidential stationery that, among other things (he had seen a screen test), "your teeth require proper attention with polishing and cleaning by a dentist once every two months and very careful attention several times daily. It should be a practice of yours to open your mouth a little wider when you smile so that your teeth are seen more."

These considerations had not been important previously. Mix had changed that. Buck proved popular with audiences and kept Mix in line (although he did get his seventeen thousand dollars a week) as long as they were both at Fox. None of Buck's Westerns from this period survive. As might be expected, Mix was at first rather hostile. Later, during the sound era, the two became close friends.

The finest Mix film we have is *Rider of Death Valley*, made in 1932 by Universal, one of nine all-talking Westerns Mix did before he quit pictures altogether. His return in 1935 for Mascot's *The Miracle Rider*, a fifteen-chapter serial, was an indifferent affair done strictly to finance the Tom Mix Circus. I rank *Rider of Death Valley* with *The Vanishing American* (Paramount, 1927) in which Lois Wilson was also the heroine, *Stagecoach, My Darling Clementine, Shane* (Paramount, 1953) and *True Grit* (Paramount, 1969) as a film just short of perfection, without pretension and what's more—as with the others—capable of being enthusiastically enjoyed by an audience that does not like Westerns. The principals, including Mix, Miss Wilson and Fred Kohler, Sr., find themselves stranded in the desert without water fighting a desperate battle against the elements. The simple drama of its story inspired the later *Treasure of the Sierra Madre* (Warner's, 1948). Daniel Clark was the cameraman. Every shot is masterful with a sustaining poetry. I find it exceedingly fortunate that one of Mix's brightest moments should be preserved so that future generations can realize that his reputation and fame were not unjustified.

Also among survivors, beyond a handful of Mix films, are two exceptional John Ford vehicles of the silent era, *The Iron Horse* (Fox, 1924) and *3 Bad Men* (Fox, 1926). The land-rush sequence from *3 Bad Men*, as that in the two makes of Edna Ferber's *Cimarron*, was probably suggested by *Tumbleweeds*, Hart's only epic.

Universal competed with their Hoot Gibson series, Gibson like Buck Jones stressing a comic, offhand, seldom serious approach to the Western format. When sound came, Jones became serious (a total bankruptcy not of his own doing was a contributing factor) and revealed himself to be an actor as well as a capable action player. Gibson never changed, to his detriment. Beginning with *The Red Rider* (Universal,

1934), a serial, Buck made his best sound films in the mid-Thirties for Universal. Compact, intelligent Westerns with a mature appeal that is still evident, entries like *The Ivory-Handled Guns, Ride 'Em Cowboy* (the story to which Buck wrote), *Sudden Bill Dorn, Left-handed Law* and *Smoke Tree Range* constitute a substantial legacy. Amid the fantastic proliferation of low-order "B" Westerns, they gleam like rare gems. I could wish the same had been true of Hoot Gibson. Perhaps only *Cowboy Counsellor* (Allied, 1932) and *The Fighting Parson* (Allied, 1932) contain a glimmer of the quality of his silent Universal Jewels and Specials.

I am puzzled by those critics who claim that Ken Maynard's most outstanding Westerns were his silent series for First National. Only 1927's *The Red Raiders* survives—admittedly an excellent film—and five of six reels of *Somewhere in Sonora* (First National, 1927). I would opt for *Wheels of Destiny* (Universal, 1934), which I had Universal reissue, and *Strawberry Roan* (Universal, 1933). The latter was built around Curley Fletcher's popular ballad and gave rise to the musical Westerns of the Thirties and Forties.

From what we have left of them, the films in Paramount's Zane Grey series from 1925–39 may easily have been the most consistently impressive Westerns ever made not centered around a single personality (save a loose connection with Grey). This series went from the heights of *The Vanishing American* to the brilliant *Man of the Forest* (Paramount, 1933), directed by Henry Hathaway. Throughout, the entries were remarkable.

I cannot hope to describe the hundreds of moderately budgeted Westerns made up to 1954, or the serials, or many of the specials that might be worth viewing again. Republic developed an extremely resilient formula for what could be called "standard" Westerns, as did Columbia. Many of the Republics are as thrilling today as then, as in the case of *The Gay Caballero*, a 1936 resumption of Zorro, or *Riders of Whistling Skull* (Republic, 1936), based on William Colt MacDonald's Three Mesquiteer book of the same title, a series begun by RKO in 1935 with *Powdersmoke Range* starring Harry Carey, Hoot Gibson, Tom Tyler, Bob Steele and a plethora of other Western performers. On a $750,000 budget in 1940, Republic inaugurated with *Dark Command* a program of one big Western a year that united their incredibly slick production techniques with fascinating stories and top-flight casts. *Hell-Fire* from 1947, for instance, proved that Bill Elliott was adept at more than being "Wild Bill" or "Red Ryder."

As convenient as it might be to comment that the "B" Western ended in 1954 with Allied Artists' *Two Guns and a Badge,* in truth it happened much earlier, perhaps already by 1940. The "B" Westerns after World War II just aren't as carefully made as those from before. Gene Autry's Columbia features during the years 1947–53 are somewhat of an exception, as are the Tim Holt RKO series and several Republic entries. But on the whole, the passion and dedication expended in the "B" units in the Twenties and Thirties were generally confined thenceforth to major productions. I will confess to the reader my suspicion that neither Producers' Releasing Corporation nor Monogram ever made a notable Western.

In behalf of the "B" product of the Thirties—the Universal films with Mix, Maynard and Jones, the Columbia features with Buck Jones and Tim McCoy, the RKO George O'Brien series, the Republic Westerns with John Wayne and the Three Mesquiteers—let me say this. In many ways they achieved a uniquely American perfection of the well-made story that would be the equal in France of Guy de Maupassant's tales or of W. Somerset Maugham's short stories in English. The French say, *"Le style est l'homme même."* Nowhere is that more true than of these—permit me—cowboy pictures. Dramatists since the Greeks and the Hebrew prophets have not been fools. The tradition of a story of classic proportion with a beginning, middle and suspenseful ending has pleased the public for twenty centuries. It did so again here, albeit briefly and unexpectedly.

V

In order to better assess Westerns since 1945, critics tend to discount actors and concentrate on directors. I do not object to the practice but I do wish to remind the reader that this is only an artificial methodology. It comes not as a result of observation but rather as a framework *for* observation. In this shift of emphasis, it is nonetheless true that a director is not necessarily merely as good as his last picture, whereas an actor very well might be. A successful Western is still dependent on many elements besides its director, one of these being star attraction, a fact widely accepted in the industry but begrudgingly outside of it.

I am not saying that at times a director's influence isn't decisive. You need only look at *Frontier Marshal* (20th Century-Fox, 1939) with Randolph Scott and contrast it with John Ford's remake, *My Darling Clementine* (20th Century-Fox, 1946). Ford's film is a masterpiece. No scene is extraneous; sentiment is never sticky; it does not sag in the middle. Everything pushes forward to the shoot-out; nothing distracts. The characters exude confrontation with savagery and sudden death. Yet, there is humor and humanity and friendship and hope. Together with *Stagecoach,* I believe it Ford's finest work in the genre.

In part, Ford was working from what Wyatt Earp had told him. He knew the effects he wanted to get—and he brought them off. He brilliantly recreated the polarities, the emotions around an historical event, and meticulously etched the sensibilities involved. It has the incomparable virtue of brevity and the white heat of unflagging inspiration —the players, the technical crew, the screenplay are transfixed by the personal vision of the director. But it isn't always so. To erect a cult around only a director is to obfuscate a thousand contributing nuances. Far more noteworthy in evaluating *Western Union* (20th Century-Fox, 1941) is the fact that Harry Joe Brown was the associate producer—he had supervised or directed Maynard's First National and Universal 1929–30 Westerns—than that Fritz Lang directed it.

Because of the disparateness of the post-1945 Westerns I cannot possibly condense them into so limited a space as I have at my disposal. Eschewing the *auteur* syndrome of organization, I think it is still possible to discern two distinct trends. One was summed up by Sam Peckinpah when he said, "The Western is a universal frame within which it is possible to comment on today." The other was formulated by Howard Hawks: "To me a Western is gunplay and horses. . . . They're about adventurous life and sudden death. It's the most dramatic thing you can do."

You may feel the Peckinpah principle didactic, extreme, an imposition. I will admit that in practice it is much like going to see a Bernard Shaw play and getting the preface read to you first, and sometimes not seeing the play at all. But whatever, it has its proponents. The essential notion is "today." Authenticity and history can be warped to serve contemporary causes as much as they have been warped to provide entertainment or articulate a mythology.

I do not deny the power of Stanley Kramer's *High Noon*. It is an excellent film and deserves the awards it won. Gary Cooper's resigned but desperate persistence; Dimitri Tiomkin's music, and especially the ballad sung by Tex Ritter; the editing, which is ingenious—these are factors that must receive their due. But setting the story in the Old West is irrelevant. It is a Western only incidentally. *The Chase* (Columbia, 1966) with Marlon Brando is an even more telling presentation of America's virulent social decay in a modern Texas township. For me, *The Chase* makes the issues at hand more immediate. I know Bertholt Brecht said that optimally effective social criticism requires a sense of distance as a protection. I cannot entirely agree. If it's criticism of present-day society that you have in mind, perhaps *High Noon's* pastness is an indulgence in escapism we should deny ourselves. Our ancestors may have had a lot of festering problems, but cowardice and indecision were scarcely foremost among them.

High Noon fits Peckinpah's principle. Ultimately, whether or not you can accept such incongruities with equanimity is a matter of taste. There have been numerous Westerns socially relevant to the period depicted and not without significance now. *The Ox-Bow Incident* (20th Century-Fox, 1943), directed by William Wellman and starring

Henry Fonda, is a splendid instance. *Silver Lode* (RKO, 1953), directed by Allan Dwan and featuring John Payne and Lizabeth Scott, is another. These films indict society as the villain; they avoid the black and white morality of traditional Westerns. No performance in either of them can surpass Gary Cooper's in *High Noon*, but their shared basic premise derives from their natural setting rather than being imposed upon it.

Howard Hawks' *Rio Bravo* (Warner's, 1959), although a total antithesis to *High Noon*, is, ironically, as much a ready candidate for the directors' cults as Peckinpah's *Ride the High Country* (M-G-M, 1962). Duke Wayne plays a sheriff who, by superiority to his environment and fundamental heroism, can inspire men to rally around him. I believe it is an important distinction to make that in both *High Noon* and *The Chase*, the sheriff protagonist walks away from his job at the conclusion. In *Rio Bravo*, that is not a feasible alternative. I am reminded of Gary Merrill's comment in *Mysterious Island* (Columbia, 1961) upon arrival at Captain Nemo's retreat, "When are we going to stop escaping *to* places that need escaping *from?*"

John Ford is of the opinion that *Stagecoach* made Duke a star, but that Hawks' *Red River* (United Artists, 1948) made him an actor. Hawks has no response to this. But he did tell Wayne when he wanted him to play the part of Tom Dunson, "You're *gonna* be an old man pretty soon, and you ought to get used to it. And you also better start playing characters instead of that junk you've been playing." Short of *True Grit*, it's Wayne's best Western.

Henry Hathaway is frequently underrated. This may be due in large measure to the unavailability of many of his fine Westerns of the Thirties. There is a generating line of sorts that unifies *The Thundering Herd* (Paramount, 1933) with Harry Carey and Randolph Scott, *Man of the Forest* with these same principals, *Go West, Young Man* (Paramount, 1936) with Mae West and Randolph Scott, *Shepherd of the Hills* (Paramount, 1941) with Duke and Carey and *True Grit* (Paramount, 1969). His Westerns are marked by a cognizance of human isolation and his heroes by a stubborn *Innigkeit* (interiorality). More than a little of Ford's personal irascibility crept into Duke's Rooster Cogburn.

What most of us are inclined to overlook in connection with the Westerns made since the war is the separation of generations. The players and directors who were working in the industry prior to 1945 belong to a rough-and-tumble world where a man with talent could cut a deep niche for himself in his profession. For them the United States has been a land of nearly unlimited opportunity and they are openly grateful. For those since, they've made as much money; they've had as many—or more—opportunities. But their films reflect unhappiness. In several cases they've had sufficient control that—should the reader be so inclined—by viewing and analyzing their films, while you may not be entertained, you should be able to distill the multiple sources of their unhappiness.

VI

The romantic view of the American Indian as a godlike pagan, a fierce but untutored ally in whom barbarism, while deplorable, is wholly forgiven due to his childish simplicity, has been propounded by many film makers. Maurice Tourneur's *The Last of the Mohicans* (Associated Producers, 1920) is one such example. Thomas Ince, as early as *The Invaders* (Bison, 1912), was touched by the spectacle of a crushed Indian civilization. Colonel Tim McCoy, who worked as an Indian agent in Wyoming, became technical consultant first on *The Covered Wagon* and then on *The Vanishing American*. If the trades of the Twenties are to be believed, the latter is more compelling today than at the time of its initial release.

It is now the custom to point to these films, and perhaps to McCoy's own vehicles *War Paint* (M-G-M, 1926) and *Winners of the Wilderness* (M-G-M, 1927), as rare incidences of compassion amid hundreds of Westerns picturing Indians as mindless savages. Other critics call attention to *Broken Arrow* (20th Century-Fox, 1950) as a renewal of this trend right down to the anti-white-man films of the Seventies. Of course this assertion entirely ignores features like Tim McCoy's *End of the Trail* (Columbia, 1932) or Gene Autry's *The Cowboy and the Indians* (Columbia, 1949) which fall during the decades of ostensible "neglect" and are exceedingly moving in their sympathies—directly from the "B" units where you'd least anticipate finding them.

Critical barnstorming in this manner strikes me as ill-advised. Most often a pro-Indian picture breaks one cliché in order to foster another. Men like Tim McCoy with whom I have spoken, who have lived among Indians and learned their languages, know best the difference between Indians in real life and Indians on the screen. When Tim signed at Metro, W. S. Van Dyke, the director on his early pictures, sat down with him and said, "Now, Tim, tell me about the Indians. Just talk about them. Everything you know about them." Van Dyke wanted an interesting story with popular appeal. He got it.

Uncle Carl Laemmle kept Chief Thunderbird, Chief Big Tree and All-American Jim Thorpe under contract at Universal for years. From them he got "zany savages" movies by the bushel such as the serials *The Indians Are Coming* (Universal, 1930) with McCoy and *Battling with Buffalo Bill* (Universal, 1931). Uncle Carl's Indians were happy to be working and in their way did their best to put together an exhilarating cinematic story. The preponderantly Jewish management of the film industry would have, perhaps, predisposed executives to promote tolerance had that been an issue. It wasn't.

About the time of Sam Fuller's *Run of the Arrow* (RKO, 1956)— comparable in the sound era to the silent *Vanishing American*—the impulse for social criticism in filmmaking began addressing itself increasingly to the Indian problem. You can get away with it, if you're subtle, and it has brought about several memorable Westerns. But you can never forget your audience. Pre-1945 audiences were inclined to look upon Indians as appropriate villains without any consciousness of prejudice. The celluloid battles were just a further evolution of the routines of the Wild West shows and what I might term the "Buffalo Bill approach" to history: namely, the taller the tale, the more exciting, the more spectacular, the better. Modern audiences in the under-thirty group now demand—so say some film makers—that values be reversed, hypocrisies exposed. So it goes in the other direction. But with *Love Story* in 1969 and *The Godfather* in 1972, Paramount has proven indisputably that audiences will enthusiastically embrace the most incredible soap opera and that the American amusement at criminal violence is as strong as ever.

Audiences are mercurial. You can't tell from one week to the next what notion is going to have mass support and critical endorsement. Gene Autry, whose aptitude for business has been well demonstrated, recently bought all rights to his old Republic Westerns and opines that there is a substantial market for them. Others feel that what the Western needs (as proven by the popularity of the so-called "Spaghetti" variety) is yet more violence and, above all, more sex. The only constant in every one of these trends is the Western setting.

If I were compelled to select a single Western that does justice to both sides of the Indian wars—to both the inevitability and the tragedy—it would be *Fort Apache* (RKO, 1948). In it the cavalry is not painted in the hues of H. G. Wells' Martians with "intelligences vast, cool and unsympathetic," chopping down the Indians for economic, ecological or any other reasons; nor are the Indians perceived as innocent children disturbed in a romp through Paradise. Civilizations, like religions, have a curious way of ignoring the rights of others to be contrary.

Duke Wayne's *Hondo* (Warner's, 1954) employs a similarly balanced perspective. "Too bad," says Duke, faced with the outcome of Indian tribal existence. "It was a good way of life."

But then, as I suspect I may have made obvious, whether the picture playing is Griffith's *The Birth of a Nation* or Stanley Kramer's *High Noon* or anything since, one does not go to the movies—and Westerns most of all—to obtain either a balanced view or accurate history.

VII

For me the chronicle of the Western picture is very much a chronicle of the lives, passions, struggles and beliefs of the men who made the films. I regret that I have not been able to say more about them as people. They have had an enduring, unshakable love affair with the land and the spirit of the men who pioneered it. We're busy substituting outer space today because we've reached the ocean and can go no further. We are an urban culture enraptured by an agrarian dream of the past, precious to us because of the hope it held out.

Let me take you to Durango, Mexico. It is just after Christmas, 1972. Two production companies are here shooting Westerns. Sam Peckinpah is remaking *One-Eyed Jacks* (Paramount, 1961). It is a director's picture. M-G-M proposes to release it as *Billy the Kid and Pat Garrett*. This is going to be no fantasy like Metro's 1930 entry with Johnny Mack Brown or their remake in 1942 with Robert Taylor. "This is the real story," Peckinpah asserts.

Duke Wayne is filming *Cahill, U.S. Marshal* for Warner's. Andrew McLaglen, Victor's son, is the nominal director. Duke, however, is everywhere on the set, giving orders. The Peckinpah camp is quiet. There are few reporters around. Most of Peckinpah's company hitch a ride home for the holidays on Duke's chartered plane. "If you haven't that much money to spend," Duke says, "I don't think you should make the picture."

Duke is surrounded by reporters, answering questions between scenes. The reporters are not friendly. They bait Duke. It is their hope that he'll make a slip, some political comment they can lampoon. Reporters, like critics, have usually felt themselves superior to the subject at hand.

"What do you think of Kissinger?"

"There is a very fine dust in here," Duke remarks, coughing. It is a dry cough; there is no phlegm. Duke lives on only a part of a lung. "Can you see the dust up there, a fine white dust?"

"Do you smoke very much?"

"Only three cigars a day. I try to keep it down."

He has smoked more than that while answering questions.

"What do you think of Kissinger?"

"Do you inhale?"

"I try not to but . . . that's hard for an inveterate smoker, but I try not to."

Duke speaks very slowly; he is relaxed. He does not impress you as being a complicated man.

"Did your doctor tell you about the cancer right away?"

"No, he didn't have the guts. He wouldn't tell me. I was going through the pictures [X rays] with an intern. He showed me the latest one of my lungs. 'This is the cancer,' he said. Then he looked at me. 'Didn't your doctor tell you?' "

"How did you feel when you found out?"

"Like somebody had hit me in the stomach with a baseball bat."

"What did you think about?"

"Well, I have enough faith in that Man up there. I thought about my family, about what they would do without me, about getting my things in order."

"Have you met Kissinger?"

This reporter has been at it for an hour. Duke has answered others' questions. He is not irritated.

"Yes."

"What did you think of him?"

Duke is cautious.

"I felt he was a nice man."

"Why did you start smoking again?" another asks.

"I used to chew but it began to affect my voice."

"What do you think of Kissinger?"

It is enough. We must leave Durango, for my time is nearly gone. André Gide tells us in *L'Immoralist,* "Les plus belles oeuvres des hommes sont obstinément douloureuses." The contradictory dynamic of our Western civilization is ambivalence. What Western man needs, and loves, he destroys. Perhaps the Western with just villains, so fashionable now, is only possible because of the heroic tradition. But traditions, like the men who create them, die.

I cannot tell you if the Western will survive without heroes. Can you tell me if Western man will survive without them?

WHAT IS A WESTERN?

Movie Chronicle: The Westerner
by ROBERT WARSHOW

*They that have power to hurt and will
    do none,
That do not do the thing they most
    do show,
Who, moving others, are themselves as
    stone,
Unmoved, cold, and to temptation slow;
They rightly do inherit heaven's graces,
And husband nature's riches from
    expense;
They are the lords and owners of their
    faces,
Others but stewards of their excellence.*

The two most successful creations of American movies are the gangster and the Westerner: men with guns. Guns as physical objects, and the postures associated with their use, form the visual and emo-

From The Immediate Experience (*Garden City, N.Y.: Doubleday and Company, Inc., 1962*), *pp. 135–54. Reprinted by permission of Paul Warshow.*

tional center of both types of films. I suppose this reflects the importance of guns in the fantasy life of Americans; but that is a less
illuminating point than it appears to be. . . .

The Western hero . . . is a figure of repose. He resembles the
gangster in being lonely and to some degree melancholy. But his
melancholy comes from the "simple" recognition that life is unavoid-
ably serious, not from the disproportions of his own temperament.
And his loneliness is organic, not imposed on him by his situation
but belonging to him intimately and testifying to his completeness.
The gangster must reject others violently or draw them violently to
him. The Westerner is not thus compelled to seek love; he is prepared to accept it, perhaps, but he never asks of it more than it can
give, and we see him constantly in situations where love is at best an
irrelevance. If there is a woman he loves, she is usually unable to
understand his motives; she is against killing and being killed, and
he finds it impossible to explain to her that there is no point in being
"against" these things: they belong to his world.

Very often this woman is from the East and her failure to understand represents a clash of cultures. In the American mind, refinement, virtue, civilization, Christianity itself, are seen as feminine, and
therefore women are often portrayed as possessing some kind of deeper
wisdom, while the men, for all their apparent self-assurance, are fundamentally childish. But the West, lacking the graces of civilization,
is the place "where men are men"; in Western movies, men have the
deeper wisdom and the women are children. Those women in the
Western movies who share the hero's understanding of life are prostitutes (or, as they are usually presented, barroom entertainers)—women,
that is, who have come to understand in the most practical way how
love can be an irrelevance, and therefore "fallen" women. The gangster, too, associates with prostitutes, but for him the important things
about a prostitute are her passive availability and her costliness: she
is part of his winnings. In Western movies, the important thing about
a prostitute is her quasi-masculine independence: nobody owns her,
nothing has to be explained to her, and she is not, like a virtuous
woman, a "value" that demands to be protected. When the Westerner
leaves the prostitute for a virtuous woman—for love—he is in fact for-
saking a way of life, though the point of the choice is often obscured
by having the prostitute killed by getting into the line of fire.

The Westerner is *par excellence* a man of leisure. Even when he
wears the badge of a marshal or, more rarely, owns a ranch, he appears
to be unemployed. We see him standing at a bar, or playing poker—
a game which expresses perfectly his talent for remaining relaxed in
the midst of tension—or perhaps camping out on the plains on some
extraordinary errand. If he does own a ranch, it is in the background;

we are not actually aware that he owns anything except his horse, his guns, and the one worn suit of clothing which is likely to remain unchanged all through the movie. It comes as a surprise to see him take money from his pocket or an extra shirt from his saddlebags. As a rule we do not even know where he sleeps at night and don't think of asking. Yet it never occurs to us that he is a poor man; there is no poverty in Western movies, and really no wealth either: those great cattle domains and shipments of gold which figure so largely in the plots are moral and not material quantities, not the objects of contention but only its occasion. Possessions too are irrelevant.

Employment of some kind—usually unproductive—is always open to the Westerner, but when he accepts it, it is not because he needs to make a living, much less from any idea of "getting ahead." Where could he want to "get ahead" to? By the time we see him, he is already "there": he can ride a horse faultlessly, keep his countenance in the face of death, and draw his gun a little faster and shoot it a little straighter than anyone he is likely to meet. These are sharply defined acquirements, giving to the figure of the Westerner an apparent moral clarity which corresponds to the clarity of his physical image against his bare landscape; initially, at any rate, the Western movie presents itself as being without mystery, its whole universe comprehended in what we see on the screen.

Much of this apparent simplicity arises directly from those "cinematic" elements which have long been understood to give the Western theme its special appropriateness for the movies: the wide expanses of land, the free movement of men on horses. As guns constitute the visible moral center of the Western movie, suggesting continually the possibility of violence, so land and horses represent the movie's material basis, its sphere of action. But the land and the horses have also a moral significance: the physical freedom they represent belongs to the moral "openness" of the West—corresponding to the fact that guns are carried where they can be seen. (And, as we shall see, the character of land and horses changes as the Western film becomes more complex.)

The gangster's world is less open, and his arts not so easily identifiable as the Westerner's. Perhaps he too can keep his countenance, but the mask he wears is really no mask: its purpose is precisely to make evident the fact that he desperately wants to "get ahead" and will stop at nothing. Where the Westerner imposes himself by the appearance of unshakable control, the gangster's pre-eminence lies in the suggestion that he may at any moment lose control; his strength is not in being able to shoot faster or straighter than others, but in being more willing to shoot. "Do it first," says Scarface expounding his mode of operation, "and keep on doing it!" With the Westerner, it is a crucial point of honor *not* to "do it first"; his gun remains in its holster until the moment of combat.

There is no suggestion, however, that he draws the gun reluctantly. The Westerner could not fulfill himself if the moment did not finally come when he can shoot his enemy down. But because that moment is so thoroughly the expression of his being, it must be kept pure. He will not violate the accepted forms of combat though by doing so he could save a city. And he can wait. "When you call me that—smile!" —the villain smiles weakly, soon he is laughing with horrible joviality, and the crisis is past. But it is allowed to pass because it must come again: sooner or later Trampas will "make his play," and the Virginian will be ready for him.

What does the Westerner fight for? We know he is on the side of justice and order, and of course it can be said he fights for these things. But such broad aims never correspond exactly to his real motives; they only offer him his opportunity. The Westerner himself, when an explanation is asked of him (usually by a woman), is likely to say that he does what he "has to do." If justice and order did not continually demand his protection, he would be without a calling. Indeed, we come upon him often in just that situation, as the reign of law settles over the West and he is forced to see that his day is over; those are the pictures which end with his death or with his departure for some more remote frontier. What he defends, at bottom, is the purity of his own image—in fact his honor. This is what makes him invulnerable. When the gangster is killed, his whole life is shown to have been a mistake, but the image the Westerner seeks to maintain can be presented as clearly in defeat as in victory: he fights not for advantage and not for the right, but to state what he is, and he must live in a world which permits that statement. The Westerner is the last gentleman, and the movies which over and over again tell his story are probably the last art form in which the concept of honor retains its strength.

Of course I do not mean to say that ideas of virtue and justice and courage have gone out of culture. Honor is more than these things: it is a style, concerned with harmonious appearances as much as with desirable consequences, and tending therefore toward the denial of life in favor of art. "Who hath it? he that died o' Wednesday." On the whole, a world that leans to Falstaff's view is a more civilized and even, finally, a more graceful world. It is just the march of civilization that forces the Westerner to move on; and if we actually had to confront the question it might turn out that the woman who refuses to understand him is right as often as she is wrong. But we do not confront the question. Where the Westerner lives it is always about 1870 —not the real 1870, either, or the real West—and he is killed or goes away when his position becomes problematical. The fact that he continues to hold our attention is evidence enough that, in his proper frame, he presents an image of personal nobility that is still real for us.

Clearly, this image easily becomes ridiculous: we need only look at William S. Hart or Tom Mix, who in the wooden absoluteness of their virtue represented little that an adult could take seriously; and doubtless such figures as Gene Autry or Roy Rogers are no better, though I confess I have seen none of their movies. Some film enthusiasts claim to find in the early, unsophisticated Westerns a "cinematic purity" that has since been lost; this idea is as valid, and finally as misleading, as T. S. Eliot's statement that *Everyman* is the only play in English that stays within the limitations of art. The truth is that the Westerner comes into the field of serious art only when his moral code, without ceasing to be compelling, is seen also to be imperfect. The Westerner at his best exhibits a moral ambiguity which darkens his image and saves him from absurdity; this ambiguity arises from the fact that, whatever his justifications, he is a killer of men.

In *The Virginian,* which is an archetypal Western movie as *Scarface* or *Little Caesar* are archetypal gangster movies, there is a lynching in which the hero (Gary Cooper), as leader of a posse, must supervise the hanging of his best friend for stealing cattle. With the growth of American "social consciousness," it is no longer possible to present a lynching in the movies unless the point is the illegality and injustice of the lynching itself; *The Ox-Bow Incident,* made in 1943, explicitly puts forward the newer point of view and can be regarded as a kind of "anti-Western." But in 1929, when *The Virginian* was made, the present inhibition about lynching was not yet in force; the justice, and therefore the necessity, of the hanging is never questioned—except by the schoolteacher from the East, whose refusal to understand serves as usual to set forth more sharply the deeper seriousness of the West. The Virginian is thus in a tragic dilemma where one moral absolute conflicts with another and the choice of either must leave a mortal stain. If he had chosen to save his friend, he would have violated the image of himself that he had made essential to his existence, and the movie would have had to end with his death, for only by his death could the image have been restored. Having chosen instead to sacrifice his friend to the higher demands of the "code"—the only choice worthy of him, as even the friend understands—he is none the less stained by the killing, but what is needed now to set accounts straight is not his death but the death of the villain Trampas, the leader of the cattle thieves, who had escaped the posse and abandoned the Virginian's friend to his fate. Again the woman intervenes: Why must there be *more* killing? If the hero really loved her, he would leave town, refusing Trampas's challenge. What good will it be if

Trampas should kill him? But the Virginian does once more what he "has to do," and in avenging his friend's death wipes out the stain on his own honor. Yet his victory cannot be complete: no death can be paid for and no stain truly wiped out; the movie is still a tragedy, for though the hero escapes with his life, he has been forced to confront the ultimate limits of his moral ideas.

This mature sense of limitation and unavoidable guilt is what gives the Westerner a "right" to his melancholy. It is true that the gangster's story is also a tragedy—in certain formal ways more clearly a tragedy than the Westerner's—but it is a romantic tragedy, based on a hero whose defeat springs with almost mechanical inevitability from the outrageous presumption of his demands: the gangster is *bound* to go on until he is killed. The Westerner is a more classical figure, self-contained and limited to begin with, seeking not to extend his dominion but only to assert his personal value, and his tragedy lies in the fact that even this circumscribed demand cannot be fully realized. Since the Westerner is not a murderer but (most of the time) a man of virtue, and since he is always prepared for defeat, he retains his inner invulnerability and his story need not end with his death (and usually does not); but what we finally respond to is not his victory but his defeat.

Up to a point, it is plain that the deeper seriousness of the good Western films comes from the introduction of a realism, both physical and psychological, that was missing with Tom Mix and William S. Hart. As lines of age have come into Gary Cooper's face since *The Virginian,* so the outlines of the Western movie in general have become less smooth, its background more drab. The sun still beats upon the town, but the camera is likely now to take advantage of this illumination to seek out more closely the shabbiness of buildings and furniture, the loose, worn hang of clothing, the wrinkles and dirt of the faces. Once it has been discovered that the true theme of the Western movie is not the freedom and expansiveness of frontier life, but its limitations, its material bareness, the pressures of obligation, then even the landscape itself ceases to be quite the arena of free movement it once was, but becomes instead a great empty waste, cutting down more often than it exaggerates the stature of the horseman who rides across it. We are more likely now to see the Westerner struggling against the obstacles of the physical world (as in the wonderful scenes on the desert and among the rocks in *The Last Posse*) than carelessly surmounting them. Even the horses, no longer the "friends" of man or the inspired chargers of knight-errantry, have lost much of the moral significance that once seemed to belong to them in their careering across the screen. It seems to me the horses grow tired and stumble more often than they did, and that we see them less frequently at the gallop.

In *The Gunfighter*, a remarkable film of a couple of years ago, the landscape has virtually disappeared.* Most of the action takes place indoors, in a cheerless saloon where a tired "bad man" (Gregory Peck) contemplates the waste of his life, to be senselessly killed at the end by a vicious youngster setting off on the same futile path. The movie is done in cold, quiet tones of gray, and every object in it—faces, clothing, a table, the hero's heavy mustache—is given an air of uncompromising authenticity, suggesting those dim photographs of the nineteenth-century West in which Wyatt Earp, say, turns out to be a blank untidy figure posing awkwardly before some uninteresting building. This "authenticity," to be sure, is only aesthetic; the chief fact about nineteenth-century photographs, to my eyes at any rate, is how stonily they refuse to yield up the truth. But that limitation is just what is needed: by preserving some hint of the rigidity of archaic photography (only in tone and décor, never in composition), *The Gunfighter* can permit us to feel that we are looking at a more "real" West than the one the movies have accustomed us to—harder, duller, less "romantic" —and yet without forcing us outside the boundaries which give the Western movie its validity.

We come upon the hero of *The Gunfighter* at the end of a career in which he has never upheld justice and order, and has been at times, apparently, an actual criminal; in this case, it is clear that the hero has been wrong and the woman who has rejected his way of life has been right. He is thus without any of the larger justifications, and knows himself a ruined man. There can be no question of his "redeeming" himself in any socially constructive way. He is too much the victim of his own reputation to turn marshal as one of his old friends has done, and he is not offered the sentimental solution of a chance to give up his life for some good end; the whole point is that he exists outside the field of social value. Indeed, if we were once allowed to see him in the days of his "success," he might become a figure like the gangster, for his career has been aggressively "anti-social" and the practical problem he faces is the gangster's problem: there will always be somebody trying to kill him. Yet it is obviously absurd to speak of him as "anti-social," not only because we do not see him acting as a criminal, but more fundamentally because we do not see his milieu as a society. Of course it has its "social problems" and a kind of static history: civilization is always just at the point of driving out the old freedom; there are women and children to represent the possibility of a settled life; and there is the marshal, a

* This essay was first published in 1954. ed.

bad man turned good, determined to keep at least his area of jurisdiction at peace. But these elements are not, in fact, a part of the film's "realism," even though they come out of the real history of the West; they belong to the conventions of the form, to that accepted framework which makes the film possible in the first place, and they exist not to provide a standard by which the gunfighter can be judged, but only to set him off. The true "civilization" of the Western movie is always embodied in an individual, good or bad is more a matter of personal bearing than of social consequences, and the conflict of good and bad is a duel between two men. Deeply troubled and obviously doomed, the gunfighter is the Western hero still, perhaps all the more because his value must express itself entirely in his own being—in his presence, the way he holds our eyes—and in contradiction to the facts. No matter what he has done, he *looks* right, and he remains invulnerable because, without acknowledging anyone else's right to judge him, he has judged his own failure and has already assimilated it, understanding—as no one else understands except the marshal and the barroom girl—that he can do nothing but play out the drama of the gun fight again and again until the time comes when it will be he who gets killed. What "redeems" him is that he no longer believes in this drama and nevertheless will continue to play his role perfectly: the pattern is all.

The proper function of realism in the Western movie can only be to deepen the lines of that pattern. It is an art form for connoisseurs, where the spectator derives his pleasure from the appreciation of minor variations within the working out of a pre-established order. One does not want too much novelty: it comes as a shock, for instance, when the hero is made to operate without a gun, as has been done in several pictures (e.g., *Destry Rides Again*), and our uneasiness is allayed only when he is finally compelled to put his "pacifism" aside. If the hero can be shown to be troubled, complex, fallible, even eccentric, or the villain given some psychological taint or, better, some evocative physical mannerism, to shade the colors of his villainy, that is all to the good. Indeed, that kind of variation is absolutely necessary to keep the type from becoming sterile; we do not want to see the same movie over and over again, only the same form. But when the impulse toward realism is extended into a "reinterpretation" of the West as a developed society, drawing our eyes away from the hero if only to the extent of showing him as the one dominant figure in a complex social order, then the pattern is broken and the West itself begins to be uninteresting. If the "social problems" of the frontier are to be the movie's chief concern, there is no longer any point in re-examining these problems twenty times a year; they have been solved, and the people for whom they once were real are dead. Moreover, the hero himself, still the film's central figure, now tends to become its one unassimilable element, since he is the most "unreal."

The Ox-Bow Incident, by denying the convention of the lynching, presents us with a modern "social drama" and evokes a corresponding response, but in doing so it almost makes the Western setting irrelevant, a mere backdrop of beautiful scenery. (It is significant that The Ox-Bow Incident has no hero; a hero would have to stop the lynching or be killed in trying to stop it, and then the "problem" of lynching would no longer be central.) Even in The Gunfighter the women and children are a little too much in evidence, threatening constantly to become a real focus of concern instead of simply part of the given framework; and the young tough who kills the hero has too much the air of juvenile criminality: the hero himself could never have been like that, and the idea of a cycle being repeated therefore loses its sharpness. But the most striking example of the confusion created by a too conscientious "social" realism is in the celebrated High Noon.

In High Noon we find Gary Cooper still the upholder of order that he was in The Virginian, but twenty-four years older, stooped, slower moving, awkward, his face lined, the flesh sagging, a less beautiful and weaker figure, but with the suggestion of greater depth that belongs almost automatically to age. Like the hero of The Gunfighter, he no longer has to assert his character and is no longer interested in the drama of combat; it is hard to imagine that he might once have been so youthful as to say, "When you call me that—smile!" In fact, when we come upon him he is hanging up his guns and his marshal's badge in order to begin a new, peaceful life with his bride, who is a Quaker. But then the news comes that a man he had sent to prison has been pardoned and will get to town on the noon train; three friends of this man have come to wait for him at the station, and when the freed convict arrives the four of them will come to kill the marshal. He is thus trapped; the bride will object, the hero himself will waver much more than he would have done twenty-four years ago, but in the end he will play out the drama because it is what he "has to do." All this belongs to the established form (there is even the "fallen woman" who understands the marshal's position as his wife does not). Leaving aside the crudity of building up suspense by means of the clock, the actual Western drama of High Noon is well handled and forms a good companion piece to The Virginian, showing in both conception and technique the ways in which the Western movie has naturally developed.

But there is a second drama along with the first. As the marshal sets out to find deputies to help him deal with the four gunmen, we are taken through the various social strata of the town, each group in turn refusing its assistance out of cowardice, malice, irresponsibility, or venality. With this we are in the field of "social drama"—of a very low order, incidentally, altogether unconvincing and displaying a vulgar anti-populism that has marred some other movies of Stanley Kramer's. But the falsity of the "social drama" is less important than the fact that it does not belong in the movie to begin with. The technical problem was to make it necessary for the marshal to face his enemies alone; to explain *why* the other townspeople are not at his side is to raise a question which does not exist in the proper frame of the Western movie, where the hero is "naturally" alone and it is only necessary to contrive the physical absence of those who might be his allies, if any contrivance is needed at all. In addition, though the hero of *High Noon* proves himself a better man than all around him, the actual effect of this contrast is to lessen his stature: he becomes only a rejected man of virtue. In our final glimpse of him, as he rides away through the town where he has spent most of his life without really imposing himself on it, he is a pathetic rather than a tragic figure. And his departure has another meaning as well; the "social drama" has no place for him.

But there is also a different way of violating the Western form. This is to yield entirely to its static quality as legend and to the "cinematic" temptations of its landscape, the horses, the quiet men. John Ford's famous *Stagecoach* (1938) had much of this unhappy preoccupation with style, and the same director's *My Darling Clementine* (1946), a soft and beautiful movie about Wyatt Earp, goes further along the same path, offering indeed a superficial accuracy of historical reconstruction, but so loving in execution as to destroy the outlines of the Western legend, assimilating it to the more sentimental legend of rural America and making the hero a more dangerous Mr. Deeds. (*Powder River,* a recent "routine" Western shamelessly copied from *My Darling Clementine,* is in most ways a better film; lacking the benefit of a serious director, it is necessarily more concerned with drama than with style.)

The highest expression of this aestheticizing tendency is in George Stevens' *Shane,* where the legend of the West is virtually reduced to its essentials and then fixed in the dreamy clarity of a fairy tale. There never was so broad and bare and lovely a landscape as Stevens puts before us, or so unimaginably comfortless a "town" as the little group of buildings on the prairie to which the settlers must come for their supplies and to buy a drink. The mere physical progress of the film, following the style of *A Place in the Sun,* is so deliberately graceful that everything seems to be happening at the bottom of a clear lake. The hero (Alan Ladd) is hardly a man at all, but something like the Spirit of the West, beautiful in fringed buckskins. He emerges mysteriously from the plains, breathing sweetness and a melancholy which is no longer simply the Westerner's natural response to experience but has taken on spirituality; and when he has accomplished his mission, meeting and destroying in the black figure of Jack Palance a

Spirit of Evil just as metaphysical as his own embodiment of virtue, he fades away again into the more distant West, a man whose "day is over," leaving behind the wondering little boy who might have imagined the whole story. The choice of Alan Ladd to play the leading role is alone an indication of this film's tendency. Actors like Gary Cooper or Gregory Peck are in themselves, as material objects, "realistic," seeming to bear in their bodies and their faces mortality, limitation, the knowledge of good and evil. Ladd is a more "aesthetic" object, with some of the "universality" of a piece of sculpture; his special quality is in his physical smoothness and serenity, unworldly and yet not innocent, but suggesting that no experience can really touch him. Stevens has tried to freeze the Western myth once and for all in the immobility of Alan Ladd's countenance. If *Shane* were "right," and fully successful, it might be possible to say there was no point in making any more Western movies; once the hero is apotheosized, variation and development are closed off.

Shane is not "right," but it is still true that the possibilities of fruitful variation in the Western movie are limited. The form can keep its freshness through endless repetitions only because of the special character of the film medium, where the physical difference between one object and another—above all, between one actor and another—is of such enormous importance, serving the function that is served by the variety of language in the perpetuation of literary types. In this sense, the "vocabulary" of films is much larger than that of literature and falls more readily into pleasing and significant arrangements. (That may explain why the middle levels of excellence are more easily reached in the movies than in literary forms, and perhaps also why the status of the movies as art is constantly being called into question.) But the advantage of this almost automatic particularity belongs to all films alike. Why does the Western movie especially have such a hold on our imagination?

Chiefly, I think, because it offers a serious orientation to the problem of violence such as can be found almost nowhere else in our culture. . . . The hero of a war movie is most often simply a leader, and his superiority is likely to be expressed in a denial of the heroic: you are not supposed to be brave, you are supposed to get the job done and stay alive (this too, of course, is a kind of heroic posture, but a new—and "practical"—one). At its best, the war movie may represent a more civilized point of view than the Western, and if it were not continually marred by ideological sentimentality we might hope to find it developing into a higher form of drama. But it cannot supply the values we seek in the Western.

Those values are in the image of a single man who wears a gun on his thigh. The gun tells us that he lives in a world of violence, and even that he "believes in violence." But the drama is one of self-restraint: the moment of violence must come in its own time and according to its special laws, or else it is valueless. There is little cruelty in Western movies, and little sentimentality; our eyes are not focused on the sufferings of the defeated but on the deportment of the hero. Really, it is not violence at all which is the "point" of the Western movie, but a certain image of man, a style, which expresses itself most clearly in violence. Watch a child with his toy guns and you will see: what most interests him is not (as we so much fear) the fantasy of hurting others, but to work out how a man might look when he shoots or is shot. A hero is one who looks like a hero.

Whatever the limitations of such an idea in experience, it has always been valid in art, and has a special validity in an art where appearances are everything. The Western hero is necessarily an archaic figure; we do not really believe in him and would not have him step out of his rigidly conventionalized background. But his archaicism does not take away from his power; on the contrary, it adds to it by keeping him just a little beyond the reach both of common sense and of absolutized emotion, the two usual impulses of our art. And he has, after all, his own kind of relevance. He is there to remind us of the possibility of style in an age which has put on itself the burden of pretending that style has no meaning, and, in the midst of our anxieties over the problem of violence, to suggest that even in killing or being killed we are not freed from the necessity of establishing satisfactory modes of behavior. Above all, the movies in which the Westerner plays out his role preserve for us the pleasures of a complete and self-contained drama—and one which still effortlessly crosses the boundaries which divide our culture—in a time when other, more consciously serious art forms are increasingly complex, uncertain, and ill-defined.

Savagery, Civilization and the Western Hero

by JOHN G. CAWELTI

The Western formula emerged as Amercian attitudes toward the frontier gradually underwent significant change around the middle of the nineteenth century. It was possible for Americans in the early nineteenth century to treat the frontier as a symbol of fundamental moral antitheses between man and nature, and, consequently, to use a frontier setting in fiction that engaged itself with a profound exploration of the nature and limitations of man and society. However, the redefinition of the frontier as a place where advancing civilization met a declining savagery changed the frontier setting into a locus of conflicts which were always qualified and contained by the knowledge that the advance of civilization would largely eliminate them. Or, to put it another way, the frontier setting now provided a fictional justification for enjoying violent conflicts and the expression of lawless force without feeling that they threatened the values or the fabric of society.

The social and historical aspects of setting are just as important in defining the Western formula as geography. The Western story is set at a certain moment in the development of American civilization, namely at that point when savagery and lawlessness are in decline before the advancing wave of law and order, but are still strong enough to pose a local and momentarily significant challenge. In the actual history of the West, this moment was probably a relatively brief one in any particular area. In any case, the complex clashes of different interest groups over the use of Western resources and the pattern of settlement surely involved more people in a more fundamental way than the struggle with Indians or outlaws. Nonetheless, it is the latter

Editor's title. From John G. Cawelti, The Six Gun Mystique *(Bowling Green, Ohio: Bowling Green University Popular Press, 1971), pp. 38–47. Reprinted by permission of the publisher.*

which has become central to the Western formula. The relatively brief stage in the social evolution of the West when outlaws or Indians posed a threat to the community's stability has been erected into a timeless epic past in which heroic individual defenders of law and order without the vast social resources of police and courts stand poised against the threat of lawlessness or savagery. But it is also the nature of this epic moment that the larger forces of civilized society are just waiting in the wings for their cue. However threatening he may appear at the moment, the Indian is vanishing and the outlaw about to be superseded. It is because they too represent this epic moment that we are likely to think of such novels as Cooper's *Last of the Mohicans,* Bird's *Nick of the Woods,* or more recent historical novels like Walter Edmonds' *Drums Along the Mohawk* as Westerns, though they are not set in what we have come to know as the West.

Why then has this epic moment been primarily associated in fiction with a particular West, that of the Great Plains and the mountains and deserts of the "Far West" and with a particular historical moment, that of the heyday of the open range cattle industry of the later nineteenth century? Westerns can be set at a later time—some of Zane Grey's stories take place in the twenties and some, like those of Gene Autry, Roy Rogers or "Sky King," in the present—but even at these later dates the costumes and the way of life represented tend to be that of the later nineteenth century. Several factors probably contributed to this particular fixation of the epic moment. Included among these would be the ideological tendency of Americans to see the Far West as the last stronghold of certain traditional values, as well as the peculiar attractiveness of the cowboy hero. But more important than these factors, the Western requires a means of isolating and intensifying the drama of the frontier encounter between social order and lawlessness. For this purpose, the geographic setting of the Great Plains and adjacent areas has proved particularly appropriate, especially since the advent of film and television have placed a primary emphasis on visual articulation. Four characteristics of the Great Plains topography have been especially important: its openness, its aridity and general inhospitability to human life, its great extremes of light and climate, and, paradoxically, its grandeur and beauty. These topographic features create an effective backdrop for the action of the Western because they exemplify in visual images the thematic conflict between civilization and savagery, and its resolution. In particular, the Western has come to center about the image of the isolated town or ranch or fort surrounded by the vast open grandeur of prairie or desert and connected to the rest of the civilized world by a railroad, a stagecoach, or simply a trail. This tenuous link can still be broken by the forces of lawlessness, but never permanently. We can conceive it as a possibility that the town will be swept back into

ndscape is uniquely adaptable to certain kinds of strong visual
ffects because of the sharp contrasts of light and shadow characteris-
: of an arid climate together with the topographical contrasts of
ain and mountain, rocky outcrops and flat deserts, steep bare
nyons and forested plateaus. The characteristic openness and aridity
the topography also makes the contrast between man and nature
d between wilderness and society visually strong.

Perhaps no film exploits the visual resources of the western land-
be more brilliantly than John Ford's 1939 *Stagecoach*. The film
ns on a street in one of those western shanty towns characterized
rickety false fronts. By the rushing motion of horses and wagons
g the street and by the long vista down the street and out into the
rt we are immediately made aware of the surrounding wilderness
of the central theme of movement across it which will dominate
film. This opening introduction of the visual theme of fragile
contrasted with epic wilderness will be developed throughout
lm in the contrast between the flimsy stagecoach and the magnifi-
landscape through which it moves. Similarly, the restless motion
e opening scene will be projected into the thrust of the stage-
across the landscape. This opening is followed by several brief
leading up to the departure of the stagecoach. These scenes are
: a rather breathless pace so that they do not slow down the
of motion and flight generated by the opening. Visually, they
on two aspects of the town, its dark, narrow and crowded in-
and its ramshackle sidewalks and storefronts, thus establishing
ial terms the restrictive and artificial character of town life.
the stagecoach departs on its voyage and we are plunged into
t openness and grandeur of the wilderness with the crowded
stagecoach serving as a visual reminder of the narrow town
as left behind. Ford chose to shoot the major portion of the
ch's journey in Monument Valley, a brilliant choice because
ial characteristics of that topography perfectly embody the
mixture of epic grandeur and savage hostility that the film
. The valley itself is a large, flat desert between steep hills.
ng up out of the valley floor gigantic monoliths of bare rock
e stagecoach as it winds across this vast panorama. This com-
of large open desert broken by majestic upthrusts of rock
ounded by threatening hills creates an enormously effective
vironment for the story, which centers around the way in
e artificial social roles and attitudes of the travellers break
der the impact of the wilderness. Those travellers who are
anscend their former roles are regenerated by the experience:
en doctor delivers a baby, the meek salesman shows courage,
becomes the heroine of a romance and the outlaw becomes
by stunning photographic representation of the visual con-

the desert—the rickety wooden buildings with their
fronts help express the tenuousness of the town's positi
surrounding prairie; nonetheless we do not see the to
isolated fort in hostile country, like an outpost of the
legion in *Beau Geste,* but as the advance guard of an
zation. Moreover, while the prairie or desert may
it is not hostile. Its openness, freshness and grandeur
portant role in the Western. Thus, the open prairie
serves not only as a haven of lawlessness and savager
drop of epic magnitude and even, at times, as a sour
power.

This characteristic setting reflects and helps dram
division of characters that dominates the Western
The townspeople hover defensively in their settlen
the outlaws or Indians who are associated with th
uncontrollable elements of the surrounding land
people are static and largely incapable of move
little settlement. The outlaws or savages can me
landscape. The hero, though a friend of the t
lawless power of movement in that he, like the s
and possesses skills of wilderness existence. The
hero also appears symbolically in the Western
aridity and climatic extremes the Great Plain
the hostile savagery of Indians and outlaws, w
its vistas of snow-covered peaks in the distance
and sunsets (in the purple prose of Zane Grey, f
epic courage and regenerative power of the h
spect, Western topography helps dramatize n
of characters and the thematic conflicts of the

The special openness of the topography
western desert has made it particularly expre
movement. Against the background of this
can create infinite variations of space rang
to close-ups and he can clearly articulat
various spaces. No matter how often one
inescapably effective about that scene, bel
in which a rider appears like an infinitely
a great empty horizon and then rides towa
space, just as there is a different thrill abc
horses and men plunging pell-mell fro
empty distance. Nor is there anything w
ing of suspense when the camera picks
threading their way across the middle c
the arid rocks and up the slopes of a ca
upon a group of Indians waiting in ar

trasts of desert, hills and moving stagecoach, Ford transforms the journey of the stagecoach into an epic voyage that transcends the film's rather limited romantic plot.

Costume—another feature of the Western setting—has also contributed greatly to the Western's success in film. Like topography, western costume gains effectiveness both from intrinsic interest and from the way writers and filmmakers have learned how to make it reflect character and theme. In simplest form, as in the B Westerns, costumes symbolized moral opposition. The good guy wears clean, well-pressed clothes and a white hat. The villain dressed sloppily in black. The importance of this convention, simple-minded as it was, became apparent when, to create a more sophisticated "adult" Western, directors frequently chose to dress their heroes in black. However, the tradition of western costume also contains more complex meanings. An important distinction marks off both hero and villain from the townspeople. The townspeople usually wear the ordinary street clothing associated with the later nineteenth century, suits for men and long dresses for women. On the whole this clothing is simple as compared to the more elaborate fashions of the period and this simplicity is one way of expressing the Westernness of the costume. However, in the midst of the desert, the townspeople's clothing has an air of non-utilitarian artificiality somewhat like the ubiquitous false fronts on the town itself. It is perhaps significant that even in Westerns purportedly set at a later date, the women tend to wear the full-length dresses of an earlier period.

The costumes associated with heroes and outlaws or savages are more striking. Paradoxically, they are both more utilitarian and more artificial than those of the townspeople. The cowboy's boots, tight-fitting pants or chaps, his heavy shirt and bandana, his gun, and finally his large ten-gallon hat all symbolize his adaptation to the wilderness. But utility is only one of the principles of the hero-outlaw's dress. The other is dandyism, that highly artificial love of elegance for its own sake. In the Western, dandyism sometimes takes the overt and obvious form of elaborate costumes laid over with fringes, tassels and scrollwork like a rococo drawing room. But it is more powerfully exemplified in the elegance of those beautifully tailored cowboy uniforms which John Wayne so magnificently fills out in the Westerns of John Ford and Howard Hawks.

The enormous attraction of this combination of naturalness and artifice has played a significant role in both popular and avant-garde art since the middle of the nineteenth century. Baudelaire's fascination with the dandyism of the savage which he described as "the supreme incarnation of the idea of Beauty transported into the material world," is just one indication of the nineteenth century's fascination with the mixture of savagery and elegance which has been implicit in the costume of the Western hero from the beginning. Cooper's Leatherstocking even gained his name from his costume, suggesting the extent to which this particular kind of dress excited Cooper's imagination. Like later cowboys, Leatherstocking's costume combined nature and artifice. His dress was largely made of the skins of animals and it was particularly adapted to the needs of wilderness life. Yet at the same time it was subtly ornamented with buckskin fringes and porcupine quills "after the manner of the Indians." Still, it is important to note that Leatherstocking's costume is not that of the Indians, but rather a more utilitarian wilderness version of the settler's dress. Thus, costume exemplified the mediating role of the hero between civilization and savagery. Later the formula cowboy's costume developed along the same lines. In its basic outlines it resembled town dress more than that of the Indian, yet it was more functional for movement across the plains than that of the townspeople. At the same time, the cowboy dress had a dandyish splendor and elegance lacking in the drab fashions of the town and based on Indian or Mexican models. In later Westerns, the hero shared many of these qualities with the villain, just as Leatherstocking had a touch of the Indian, despite his repeated assurances that he was "a man without a cross," i.e. actual Indian kinship. But the hero's costume still differentiated him from the savage, whether Indian or outlaw, both by its basic resemblance to civilized dress and by its greater restraint and decorum. Thus costume, like setting, expressed the transcendent and intermediate quality of the hero. By lying between two ways of life, he transcended the restrictions and limitations of both. Or, to put it another way, the Western setting and costume embody the basic escapist principle of having your cake and eating it too.

As already indicated, there are three central roles in the Western: the townspeople or agents of civilization, the savages or outlaws who threaten this first group, and the heroes who are above all "men in the middle," that is, they possess many qualities and skills of the savages, but are fundamentally committed to the townspeople. It is out of the multiple variations possible on the relationships between these groups that the various Western plots are concocted. For example, the simplest version of all has the hero protecting the townspeople from the savages, using his own savage skills against the denizens of the wilderness. A second more complex variation shows the hero initially indifferent to the plight of the townspeople and more inclined to identify himself with the savages. However, in the course of the story his position changes and he becomes the ally of the townspeople. This variation can generate a number of different plots. There is the revenge Western: a hero seeks revenge against an outlaw or Indian who has wronged him. In order to accomplish his vengeance, he rejects the pacifistic ideals of the townspeople, but in the end he discovers that he is really committed to their way of life (John Ford's *The Searchers*). Another plot based on this variation of the character relations is that of the hero who initially seeks his own selfish material gain, using his savage skills as a means to this end; but as the story progresses, he discovers his moral involvement with the townspeople and becomes their champion (cf. Anthony Mann's film *The Far Country*). It is also possible, while maintaining the system of relationships, to reverse the conclusion of the plot as in those stories where the townspeople come to accept the hero's savage mode of action (cf. John Ford's *Stagecoach* or, to a certain extent, Wister's *The Virginian*). A third variation of the basic scheme of relationships has the hero caught in the middle between the townspeople's need for his savage skills and their rejection of his way of life. This third variation, common in recent Westerns, often ends in the destruction of the hero (cf. the films *The Gunfighter* or *Invitation to a Gunfighter*) or in his voluntary exile (*Shane, High Noon, Two Rode Together*). The existence of these and many other variations suggests that the exploration of a certain pattern of relationships is more important to the Western than a particular outcome, though it is also probable that they reflect different components of the mass audience, the simpler variation being more popular with adolescents and the more complex variations successful with adults. In addition, changing cultural attitudes have something to do with the emergence of different variations, since variation two is clearly more characteristic of early twentieth century Westerns, while variation three dominates the recent "adult" Western.

The Western: Ideology and Archetype
by JIM KITSES

First of all, the western is American history. Needless to say, this
does not mean that the films are historically accurate or that they
cannot be made by Italians. More simply, the statement means that
American frontier life provides the milieu and *mores* of the western,
its wild bunch of cowboys, its straggling towns and mountain scenery.
Of course westward expansion was to continue for over a century,
the frontier throughout that period a constantly shifting belt of settlement. However, Hollywood's West has typically been, from about
1865 to 1890 or so, a brief final instant in the process. This twilight
era was a momentous one: within just its span we can count a number of frontiers in the sudden rash of mining camps, the building of
the railways, the Indian Wars, the cattle drives, the coming of the
farmer. Together with the last days of the Civil War and the exploits
of the badmen, here is the raw material of the western.

At the heart of this material, and crucial to an understanding of
the gifts the form holds out to its practitioners, is an ambiguous, mercurial concept: the idea of the West. From time immemorial the West
had beckoned to statesmen and poets, existing as both a direction and
a place, an imperialist theme and a pastoral Utopia. Great empires
developed ever westward: from Greece to Rome, from Rome to Britain, from Britain to America. It was in the West as well that the
fabled lands lay, the Elysian fields, Atlantis, El Dorado. As every
American schoolboy knows, it was in sailing on his passage to India,
moving ever westward to realize the riches of the East, that Columbus
chanced on the New World. Hand in hand with the hope of fragrant
spices and marvellous tapestries went the ever-beckoning dream of life
eternal: surely somewhere, there where the sun slept, was the fountain
of youth.

As America began to be settled and moved into its expansionist

Editor's title. From Horizons West *(Bloomington: Indiana University
Press, 1969), pp. 8–27.* © *1969 by Jim Kitses. Reprinted by permission
of Indiana University Press, and Martin Secker and Warburg Ltd.*

phases, this apocalyptic and materialist vision found new expression. In his seminal study *Virgin Land*, Henry Nash Smith has traced how the West as symbol has functioned in America's history and consciousness. Is the West a Garden of natural dignity and innocence offering refuge from the decadence of civilization? Or is it a treacherous Desert stubbornly resisting the gradual sweep of agrarian progress and community values? Dominating America's intellectual life in the nineteenth century, these warring ideas were most clearly at work in attitudes surrounding figures like Daniel Boone, Kit Carson and Buffalo Bill Cody, who were variously seen as rough innocents ever in flight from society's artifice, and as enlightened pathfinders for the new nation. A folk-hero manufactured in his own time, Cody himself succumbed towards the end of his life to the play of these concepts that so gripped the imagination of his countrymen: "I stood between savagery and civilization most all my early days."

Refracted through and pervading the genre, this ideological tension has meant that a wide range of variation is possible in the basic elements of the form. The plains and mountains of western landscape can be an inspiring and civilizing environment, a moral universe productive of the western hero, a man with a code. But this view, popularized by Robert Warshow in his famous essay, "The Westerner," is one-sided. Equally the terrain can be barren and savage, surroundings so demanding that men are rendered morally ambiguous, or wholly brutalized. In the same way, the community in the western can be seen as a positive force, a movement of refinement, order and local democracy into the wilds, or as a harbinger of corruption in the form of Eastern values which threaten frontier ways. This analysis oversimplifies in isolating the attitudes: a conceptually complex structure that draws on both images is the typical one. If Eastern figures such as bankers, lawyers and journalists are often either drunkards or corrupt, their female counterparts generally carry virtues and graces which the West clearly lacks. And if Nature's harmonies produce the upright hero, they also harbour the animalistic Indian. Thus central to the form we have a philosophical dialectic, an ambiguous cluster of meanings and attitudes that provide the traditional, thematic structure of the genre. This shifting ideological play can be described through a series of antinomies, so:

THE WILDERNESS	CIVILIZATION
The Individual:	*The Community:*
freedom	restriction
honour	institutions
self-knowledge	illusion
integrity	compromise

THE WILDERNESS	CIVILIZATION
The Individual:	*The Community:*
self-interest	*The Community:*
solipsism	democracy
Nature:	*Culture:*
purity	corruption
experience	knowledge
empiricism	legalism
pragmatism	idealism
brutalization	refinement
savagery	humanity
The West:	*The East:*
America	Europe
the frontier	America
equality	class
agrarianism	industrialism
tradition	change
the past	the future

In scanning this grid, if we compare the tops and tails of each sub-section, we can see the ambivalence at work at its outer limits: the West, for example, rapidly moves from being the spearhead of manifest destiny to the retreat of ritual. What we are dealing with here, of course, is no less than a national world-view: underlying the whole complex is the grave problem of identity that has special meaning for Americans. The isolation of a vast unexplored continent, the slow growth of social forms, the impact of an unremitting New England Puritanism obsessed with the cosmic struggle of good and evil, of the elect and the damned, the clash of allegiances to Mother Country and New World, these factors are the crucible in which American consciousness was formed. The thrust of contradictions, everywhere apparent in American life and culture, is clearest in the great literary heritage of the romantic novel that springs from Fenimore Cooper and moves through Hawthorne and Melville, Mark Twain and Henry James, Fitzgerald and Faulkner, Hemingway and Mailer. As Richard Chase has underlined in his *The American Novel and Its Tradition,* this form in American hands has always tended to explore rather than to order, to reflect on rather than to moralize about, the irreconcilables that it confronts; and where contradictions are resolved the mode is often that of melodrama or the pastoral. For failing to find a moral tone and a style of close social observation—in short, for failing to be *English*—the American novel has often had its knuckles rapped. As with literature, so with the film: the prejudice that even now persists in many quarters of criticism and education with reference to the Hollywood cinema (paramountly in America itself) flows from a similar lack of understanding.

The ideology that I have been discussing inevitably filters through many of Hollywood's genres: the western has no monopoly here. But what gives the form a particular thrust and centrality is its historical setting; its being placed at exactly that moment when options are still open, the dream of a primitivistic individualism, the ambivalence of at once beneficent and threatening horizons, still tenable. For the film-maker who is preoccupied with these motifs, the western has offered a remarkably expressive canvas.

If we stand back from the western, we are less aware of historical (or representational) elements than of form and *archetype*. This may sound platitudinous: for years critics have spoken confidently of the balletic movement of the genre, of pattern and variation, of myth. This last, ever in the air when the form is discussed, clouds the issues completely. We can speak of the genre's celebration of America, of the contrasting images of Garden and Desert, as national myth. We can speak of the parade of mythology that is mass culture, of which the western is clearly a part. We can invoke Greek and medieval myth, referring to the western hero as a latter-day knight, a contemporary Achilles. Or we can simply speak of the myth of the western, a journalistic usage which evidently implies that life is not like that. However, in strict classical terms of definition myth has to do with the activity of gods, and as such the western has no myth. Rather, it incorporates elements of *displaced* (or corrupted) myth on a scale that can render them considerably more prominent than in most art. It is not surprising that little advance is made upon the clichés, no analysis undertaken that interprets how these elements are at work within a particular film or director's career. What are the archetypal elements we sense within the genre and how do they function? As Northrop Frye has shown in his monumental *The Anatomy of Criticism*, for centuries this immensely tangled ground has remained almost wholly unexplored in literature itself. The primitive state of film criticism inevitably reveals a yawning abyss in this direction.

From the outset the western could be many things. In their anecdotal *The Western* George N. Fenin and William K. Everson have chronicled the proliferating, overlapping growth of early days: Bronco Billy Anderson's robust action melodramas, Thomas H. Ince's darker tales, W. S. Hart's more "authentic" romances, the antics of the virtuous Tom Mix, the Cruze and Ford epics of the twenties, the stunts and flamboyance of Ken Maynard and Hoot Gibson, the flood of "B"

movies, revenge sagas, serials, and so on. Experiment seems always
to have been varied and development dynamic, the pendulum swinging back and forth between opposing poles of emphasis on drama
and history, plots and spectacle, romance and "realism," seriousness
and comedy. At any point where audience response was felt the action could freeze, the industrial machine moving into high gear to
produce a cycle and, in effect, establish a minor tradition within the
form. Whatever "worked" was produced, the singing westerns of the
thirties perhaps only the most prominent example of this policy of
eclectic enterprise.

    For many students of the western Gene Autry and Roy Rogers
have seemed an embarrassing aberration. However, such a view pre-
supposes that there is such an animal as *the* western, a precise model
rather than a loose, shifting and variegated genre with many roots
and branches. The word "genre" itself, although a helpful one, is a
mixed blessing: for many the term carries literary overtones of technical *rules*. Nor is "form" any better; the western is many *forms*. Only
a pluralist vision makes sense of our experience of the genre and begins to explain its amazing vigour and adaptability, the way it moves
closer and further from our own world, brightening or darkening
with each succeeding decade. Yet over the years critics have ever tried
to freeze the genre once and for all in a definitive model of the "classical" western. Certainly it must be admitted that works such as *Shane*
and *My Darling Clementine* weld together in remarkable balance
historical reconstruction and national themes with personal drama
and archetypal elements. In his essay, "The Evolution of the Western,"
Bazin declared *Stagecoach* the summit of the form, an example of
"classic maturity," before going on to see in Anthony Mann's early
small westerns the path of further progress. Although there is a
certain logic in searching for films at the centre of the spectrum, I
suspect it is a false one and can see little value in it. Wherever defini-
tions of *the* genre movie have been advanced they have become the
weapons of generalization. Insisting on the purity of his classical
elements, Bazin dismisses "superwesterns" (*Shane, High Noon, Duel
in the Sun*) because of their introduction of interests "not endemic."
Warshow's position is similar, although his conception of the form is
narrower, a particular kind of moral and physical texture embodied
in his famous but inadequate view of the hero as "the last gentleman."
Elsewhere Mann's films have been faulted for their neurotic qualities,
strange and powerful works such as *Rancho Notorious* have been
refused entry because they are somehow "not westerns." This impulse may well be informed by a fear that unless the form is defined
precisely (which inevitably excludes) it will disappear, wraith-like,
from under our eyes. The call has echoed out over the lonely landscape
of critical endeavour: what *is* the western?

The model we must hold before us is of a varied and flexible structure, a thematically fertile and ambiguous world of historical material shot through with archetypal elements which are themselves ever in flux. In defining the five basic modes of literary fiction Northrup Frye has described myth as stories about gods; romance as a world in which men are superior both to other men and to their environment; high mimetic where the hero is a leader but subject to social criticism and natural law; low mimetic where the hero is one of us; and ironic where the hero is inferior to ourselves and we look down on the absurdity of his plight. If we borrow this scale, it quickly becomes apparent that if the western was originally rooted between romance and high mimetic (characteristic forms of which are epic and tragedy), it rapidly became open to inflection in any direction. Surely the only definition we can advance of the western hero, for example, is that he is both complete and incomplete, serene and growing, vulnerable and invulnerable, a man and a god. If at juvenile levels the action approaches the near-divine, for serious artists who understand the tensions within the genre the focus can be anywhere along the scale. In Anthony Mann there is a constant drive towards mythic quality in the hero; in Sam Peckinpah there is a rich creative play with the romantic potential; with Budd Boetticher it is the ironic mode that dominates.

The romantic mainstream that the western took on from pulp literature provided it with the stately ritual of displaced myth, the movement of a god-like figure into the demonic wasteland, the death and resurrection, the return to a paradisal garden. Within the form were to be found seminal archetypes common to all myth, the journey and the quest, the ceremonies of love and marriage, food and drink, the rhythms of waking and sleeping, life and death. But the incursions of melodrama and revenge had turned the form on its axis, the structure torn in the direction of both morality play and tragedy. Overlaying and interpenetrating the historical thematic there was an archetypal and metaphysical ideology as well. Manifest destiny was answered by divine providence, a Classical conception of fate brooding over the sins of man. Where history was localizing and authenticating archetype, archetype was stiffening and universalizing history.

The western thus was—and is—a complex variable, its peculiar alchemy allowing a wide range of intervention, choice and experiment by script-writer and director. History provides a source of epics, spectacle and action films, pictures sympathetic to the Indian, "realistic" films, even anti-westerns (Delmer Daves's *Cowboy*). From the archetypal base flow revenge films, fables, tragedies, pastorals, and a juvenile stream of product. But of course the dialectic is always at work and the elements are never pure. Much that is produced, the great bulk of it inevitably undistinguished, occupies a blurred middle ground. But for the artist of vision in *rapport* with the genre, it offers a great freedom for local concentration and imaginative play.

It is not just that in approaching the western a director has a structure that is saturated with conceptual significance: the core of meanings is in the imagery itself. Through usage and time, recurring elements anchored in the admixture of history and archetype and so central as to be termed *structural*—the hero, the antagonist, the community, landscape—have taken on an ever-present cluster of possible significances. To see a church in a movie—any film but a western— is to see a church; the camera records. By working carefully for it a film-maker can give that church meaning, through visual emphasis, context, repetitions, dialogue. But a church in a western has *a priori* a potential expressiveness rooted in the accretions of the past. In Ford's *My Darling Clementine* a half-built church appears in one brief scene: yet it embodies the spirit of pioneer America. Settlers dance vigorously on the rough planks in the open air, the flag fluttering above the frame of the church perched precariously on the edge of the desert. Marching ceremoniously up the incline towards them, the camera receding with an audacious stateliness, come Tombstone's knight and his "lady fair," Wyatt Earp and Clementine. The community are ordered aside by the elder as the couple move on to the floor, their robust dance marking the marriage ceremony that unites the best qualities of East and West. It is one of Ford's great moments.

However, the scene is not magic, but flows from an extract understanding (or intuition) of how time-honoured elements can have the resonance of an *icon*. This term, which I borrow from art history, should connote an image that both records and carries a conceptual and emotional weight drawn from a *defined* symbolic field, a tradition. Like Scripture, the western offers a world of metaphor, a range of latent content that can be made manifest depending on the film-maker's awareness and preoccupations. Thus in Boetticher's *Decision at Sundown* a marriage ceremony is completely violated by the hero who promises to kill the bridegroom by nightfall. Here the meaning flows completely from the players, in particular Randolph Scott's irrational behaviour; the church itself is devoid of meaning. In Anthony Mann churches rarely appear. In Peckinpah churches have been a saloon and a brothel, and religion in characters has masked a damaging repressiveness. If we turn to the Indian we find that, apart from the early *Seminole*, he functions in Boetticher as part of a hostile universe, no more and no less. In Mann, however, the Indian is part of the natural order and as such his slaughter stains the landscape; it is not surprising that at times he comes, like an avenging spirit, to redress the balance. In Peckinpah the Indian, ushering in the theme of savagery, brings us to the very centre of the director's world.

Central to much that I have been saying is the principle of convention. I have refrained from using the term only because it is often loosely used and might have confused the issues. At times the term is used pejoratively, implying cliché; at others it is employed to invoke a set of mystical rules that the master of the form can juggle. In this light, a western is a western is a western. If we see the term more neutrally, as an area of agreement between audience and artist with reference to the form which his art will take, it might prove useful at this stage to recapitulate the argument by summarizing the interrelated aspects of the genre that I have tried to isolate, all of which are in some measure conventional.

(a) *History*: The basic convention of the genre is that films in western guise are about America's past. The constant tension with history and the freedom it extends to script-writer and film-maker to choose their distance is a great strength.

(b) *Themes*: The precise chronology of the genre and its inheritance of contradictions fundamental to the American mind dictate a rich range of themes expressed through a series of familiar character types and conflicts (e.g., law versus the gun, sheep versus cattle). These motifs, situations and characters can be the focus for a director's interests or can supply the ground from which he will quarry what concerns him.

(c) *Archetype*: The inherent complexity and structural confusion (or the *decadence*) of the pulp literature tradition that the western drew on from the beginning meant that westerns could incorporate elements of romance, tragedy, comedy, morality play. By a process of natural commercial selection cycles emerged and began to establish a range of forms.

(d) *Icons*: As a result of mass production, the accretions of time, and the dialectic of history and archetype, characters, situations and actions can have an emblematic power. Movement on the horizon, the erection of a community, the pursuit of Indians, these have a range of possible associations. Scenes such as passing on gun-lore, bathing or being barbered, playing poker, have a latent ritualistic meaning which can be brought to the surface and inflected. The quest, the journey, the confrontation, these can take on moral or allegorical overtones.

What holds all of these elements together (and in that sense provides the basis convention) is narrative and dramatic structure. It is only through mastery of these that a film-maker can both engage his audience and order the form in a personally meaningful way. At a general level this means the understanding and control necessary for any expression of emotion in terms of film—the creating of fear, suspense, amusement, awe. However, with an art as popular as the western this must also mean a precise awareness of audience expectation with reference to a range of characters—pre-eminently hero and antagonist—and testing situations, conflicts, spectacle, landscape, physical action and violence. Fundamental to success would seem to be the understanding that the world created must be essentially fabulous. While treating situations that have their relevance for us, the form must not impinge too directly on our experience. The world that the film creates is self-contained and its own; it comments not on our life but on the actions and relationships it reveals to us. So long as the world evoked is *other*, few limitations exist. A commonplace about the form, that it is handy for exploring simple moral issues, does not survive the experience of attending to any number of works: the maturity of relationships in Robert Parrish's *Wonderful Country*, the complex moral and metaphysical rhetoric of *Johnny Guitar*, these could hardly be called simple. Nor are social and psychological elements impossible so long as they are held in a fruitful tension with the romantic thrust of the genre. *Showdown at Boot Hill*, where Charles Bronson has become a bounty hunter because he feels he is too *short*, is an unsuccessful Freudian tale. *The Left-handed Gun*, where the murder of a father-figure turns Billy the Kid anti-social and self-destructive, is a distinguished psychological tragedy. *3.10 to Yuma* and *Shane*, both maligned because of their success where the genre proper fails (i.e., with most film journalists), are honourable works. Rather than dogma, the grounds must be quality. And the challenge always is to find the dramatic structure that best serves both film-maker and audience.

THE WESTERN AS CULTURAL ARTIFACT

The Psychological Appeal for Children of the Hollywood B Western
by FREDERICK ELKIN

I

The western, with its standard plots, values, and character types is essentially fairy tale and folklore and the actors have skills completely at variance with those that we of the audience might possess. That such fanciful elements make up the western and that it has been so universally and consistently popular suggests that it appeals to our psychological predispositions. We should like to indicate some of the predispositions to which these westerns appeal, with special emphasis on children.

Our focus is primarily on children partly because the psychological

Editor's title. From Frederick Elkin, "The Psychological Appeal of the Hollywood Western," Journal of Educational Sociology, *XXIV (October 1950), pp. 79–84 (Sections 3 and 4). Reprinted by permission of the American Sociological Association and the author.*

data about them are more reliable, and partly because they are in many respects the most significant part of the western audience. Children compromise less than half of this audience, but being immature, presumably are most affected. Also a child does not just see a western, he vividly and emotionally participates in it.[1]

We shall discuss first those general psychological factors which might apply to any dramatic hero stories, for westerns are similar to hero stories of all peoples and all times; and secondly, the more specific psychological satisfactions relevant to the western itself.

There is little doubt that a child, as well as many an adult, finds the world to be a complex and confusing place. There is so much that the child does not understand and which, especially when it involves human behavior, he cannot predict. In the western—as, of course, in most hero stories—the child can imagine himself in a world that is simple, clear-cut, and well-ordered. There are no unnecessary characters, no irrelevant intrusions, no complex personalities, and no problems left unresolved. For the child who as yet makes no artistic demands, surely it is psychologically satisfying to identify with a world he can readily understand.

It is also generally agreed by child psychologists that a child has certain feelings of inferiority and insecurity. Not only does the child find it difficult to understand the big confusing world, but the world and its members can be very threatening. The child is smaller and necessarily weaker than others who can enforce their will over him. Symbolizing these threats in the western are the danger situations of the hero. The hero is invariably threatened by powerful groups of outlaws or dishonest citizens. In identifying with the confident hero of the western story, the child is reassured. No matter what the odds or the dangers, the child in his imagination can, without the slightest fear or hesitation, overcome his adversaries and affirm his own strength and importance.

It is another characteristic of the normal child that he demands some kind of imaginative activity. The child is restricted and hemmed in by the conditions of his actual life—by the smallness of his apartment, the constant demands of the school and the family, and his own weakness. In the western, the child can imaginatively escape from the enclosures and the demands and give rein to his desire for freedom. Like the hero, he becomes free to roam amidst the wide open spaces of the west, to choose his own direction and his own course of action.

---

[1] We are assuming throughout that the normal child identifies with the western hero. Considering that the hero is by far the most prominent of the characters in the western and that the child in the theater cheers the hero, feels tense when he is in danger and relieved when he is safe, this seems a justifiable assumption.

1. Jim Thorpe, "Uncle" Carl Laemmle, and Lucile Browne,
heroine of *Battling with Buffalo Bill* (Universal, 1931). Photo
courtesy of Lucile Browne Flavin.

2. The Western as American epic. The Land Rush sequence in *Cimarron* (RKO, 1931). Photo courtesy The Museum of Modern Art/Film Stills Archive.

3. The Western as American allegory. The stagecoach enters Monument Valley in *Stagecoach* (United Artists, 1939). Photo courtesy The Museum of Modern Art/Film Stills Archive. Reprinted by permission of United Artists.

4. The Western as American ritual. The Dance at the Church in *My Darling Clementine* (Twentieth Century-Fox, 1946). Photo courtesy The Museum of Modern Art/Film Stills Archive and Twentieth Century-Fox. Copyright Twentieth Century-Fox Film Corporation. All rights reserved.

5. The first Western star, G. M. (Broncho Billy) Anderson. Photo courtesy The Museum of Modern Art/Film Stills Archive.

6. King of the Teens. William S. Hart. Photo courtesy The Museum of Modern Art/Film Stills Archive.

7. King of the Twenties. Tom Mix and Tony. Photo courtesy
The Museum of Modern Art/Film Stills Archive.

8. King of the Thirties. Gene Autry. Photo courtesy The Museum of Modern Art/Film Stills Archive.

9. King of the Forties. Roy Rogers with part of his movie "Family"—Dale Evans, George "Gabby" Hayes, and Trigger. Photo courtesy The Museum of Modern Art/Film Stills Archive.

10. The new Western hero. Clint Eastwood as The Man with No Name in *A Fistful of Dollars* (United Artists, 1967). Reprinted by permission of United Artists.

11. Gary Cooper in his Academy Award winning role of Will Kane in *High Noon* (United Artists, 1952). Photo courtesy The Museum of Modern Art/Film Stills Archive. Reprinted by permission of United Artists.

12. John Wayne in his favorite role, Ethan Edwards in *The Searchers* (Warner Brothers, 1956). Photo courtesy The Museum of Modern Art/Film Stills Archive.

The child also has aggressive feelings, feelings which, according to most psychologists, are primarily a reaction to frustration. Certainly the frustrating forces are many. The child, of necessity, cannot freely express his impulses. He must, at different ages, undergo toilet training, refrain from playing with matches or pulling his sister's hair, remain quiet when he wishes to cry out, and the like. This being the case, it is psychologically satisfying for the child to have outlets for the blocked energies and impulses, and one outlet is the expression of aggression. Such aggression appears in the western in numerous chases, gun battles, and slugfests. The hero too, with whom the child identifies, is a man capable of vigorous aggressive action, such action being condoned, of course, only when he is fighting for justice. In this way, the western relieves a child's tension.

It is another important aspect of these western stories that the hero is fighting for right and justice. Thus, when the child imaginatively does these heroic and aggressive deeds, he is winning sanction from those very forces of society which make demands on him and from whom he seeks approval. In fighting for justice and in winning moral victories, the child symbolically wins the love and the admiration of his parents, teachers, and religious leaders.

Related to this type of satisfaction is the approval the child might also get from his own conscience. Having been taught a moral code of behavior which he does not completely live up to, the child may develop guilt feelings. In fighting for justice, the child can, to some degree, salve his conscience and atone for his guilty actions and thoughts.

And finally the western serves a psychological function in offering the child a choice of heroes. At a certain stage in his development the normal child will stop idealizing his one-time all-powerful parents and substitute other heroes, these heroes in turn being replaced later by others. The westerns, as well as numerous other sources, add to the choice of heroes from which the child may select.

II

In addition to these more basic gratifications offered by the western and most hero stories, a child may derive satisfactions from certain specific details of the western.

One such detail is the prominence of the horse. It has often been observed that the individual who controls a horse—a big, live, active, strong, responding animal—feels a deep sense of his own power. That a child who feels small and inferior should get such satisfaction out of a fantasy in which he owns and rides a horse seems very plausible. We leave aside any possible phallic significance.

Also this horse in many westerns is more than just a symbol of strength. For the horse, being named, glorified, and exhibited, becomes something of a personal pet. Roy Rogers' horse, for example, is "Trigger, the Smartest Horse in the Movies," and Gene Autry's is "Champion, the Wonder Horse," and both of these horses often have roles in the plot. So imaginatively the child might also have the satisfactions of the pet; the pet of whom he is proud, to whom he gives love, and from whom he can always be sure of receiving love.

Another such specific element in the western which offers psychological satisfaction is the role of the comic. First, because the hero is a close friend of the comic character, it is suggested that he, the hero, is a fine and sympathetic person. Then too, this comic is generally a flunkey who never questions the hero's authority or hesitates to obey his commands. To the child who feels that demands are always being made on him, this can be an important satisfaction; for imaginatively he can now completely dominate another human being.

The comic expresses a very simple humor and the child can also feel satisfactions similar to those of watching a circus clown. These may include the satisfactions of relieving emotional tension, of feeling superior to an adult, and of expressing aggression.

Another minor satisfaction of the western derives from the fact that the villain leader always poses as an honorable citizen. Thus, imaginatively, the scoundrel can symbolize a person one knows, dislikes, and perhaps envies, an individual whom others consider respectable. Thus to the child, the villain may symbolically represent the teacher's pet or the boy next door who dutifully practices his musical instrument. In the western, the child, identifying with the hero, always gets the satisfaction of exposing and thrashing this villain.

There are also several miscellaneous characteristics of the western which emphasize the star's heroics. The hero, for example, always fights fairly while the villains whom he defeats do not. Further, the hero is often offered positions of wealth and prestige, or in these modern westerns, the love of a beautiful girl; but the hero proudly refuses these offers, choosing to remain an independent hero of the frontier. In stressing the heroic qualities of the hero, such details build up the psychological satisfaction for the child who identifies with him.

It is another possible minor satisfaction for the American child—one that appeals to his pride—to know that it is the history of his own country that is being portrayed.

Each type of western, although following the standard pattern, does have its own peculiar characteristics and these characteristics do suggest different psychological satisfactions. Thus, Charles Starrett—like Superman of the comic strips—plays a dual role. On the one hand he is an ordinary cowboy, symbolizing what the child of the audience really is; while, on the other, he is the respected, mysterious Durango Kid, clothed in black, wearing a mask, riding a white horse, and appearing in the nick of time—symbolizing what the child would like to be.

Some westerns, especially those of Bill Boyd, alias Hopalong Cassidy and Allen "Rocky" Lane often have a mystery angle, and the suspense satisfactions of the "whodunit" become part and parcel of the western. In some westerns, the hero might be framed and the crowds turn against him. In the end, of course, his true motives are recognized and he is more than vindicated. Others have musical comedy teams; others, romances between minor characters; others, heroes who stand out because they are bullwhip experts; others, singing stars; and so on. Each type of western varies slightly in the characteristics and thereby in its potential psychological appeals.

Western Approaches:
A Note on Dialogue
by T. J. ROSS

What most instructively surprises when you juxtapose a vintage Western of the twenties with one dating from the sixties are those markings which, underlying all the differences you would expect, reveal the films' common genre. Take, for example, a characteristically swinging Western of 1961, Robert Aldrich's *The Last Sunset;* plus a Tom Mix vehicle of 1925, the silent adaptation of Zane Grey's beautifully titled pop tale, *Riders of the Purple Sage.* In his film's finale we see Mix as Lassiter the hero, together with the heroine and a young girl in her charge, all clambering on foot up a mountain pass with a gang of badmen in pursuit. Once on top, Lassiter finds that his side's only chance is to roll a great boulder down on the gang; but this would mean blocking up the only exit from the pass and so leave the couple and tot marooned indefinitely on their plateau. With the bad men closing in, the couple exchange a tense stare, till she cries (in a caption whose wording I give exactly): "I love you Lassiter—ROLL THAT STONE!"

Now in the sequel, when the trio "many years later" return to the world—no problem, they just migrate to the other side of the plateau and walk out—they can present a perfectly acceptable social unit, which is to say a unit geared to the Puritan ideal in being non-carnal and familial and chaste and productive all at the same time. (For Lassiter and his mate to have emerged after years in the hills without *anything* to show for it would have smacked of a dubious indolence; so the tot acts as necessary supplement to as well as the chaperone.) All of which looks like being light-miles away from the action of the Aldrich movie. We need only recall the scene in which Kirk Douglas

Editor's title. From T. J. Ross, "Fantasy and Form in the Western: from Hart to Peckinpah," December XII (Fall 1970), pp. 158–60. Reprinted by permission of December and the author.

woos Carol Lynley and which ends with that slow fadeout on a fren-
zied embrace which in movies means: they make out. The thing is, as
Douglas soon after learns, Lynley is his daughter by his former mistress
—and still dream girl—Dorothy Malone. The dialogue too would
seem a long way from that of the Mix opus:

Lynley: "It's a nice night, isn't it?"

Douglas (in his characteristic whinnying lilt, voice breaking on the
high note): "You miss out on your nights, you miss ha-alf your life."

The exchange has a memorable bite; especially since its calculated
hedonism, implicit in the premium placed on not "missing out," speaks
directly to present-day feelings. In contrast, the chant of I-Love-You
belongs more to the twenties; for then expectations on the average
were still tuned to that sort of concrete and essentially private and
snugly bounded experience which is posited in the chances and pre-
rogatives of True Love. For the sake of your true love story you could
otherwise risk missing out, as you cannot in a time when sex is pub-
licized as a required experience—a cool buy—for the consumer-wise;
when the sanctions, that is, are public rather than private and pro-
moted rather than dramatized. So by 1961 we hardly notice that when
Lynley ogles Douglas, it is with the single-minded passion of a neo-
phyte shopper.

Yet for all such contrasts due to time, the deeper interest of the dialogue of both films is its uniqueness to the medium. Movie dialogue
is another thing entirely from the dialogue of true life or fiction or
the stage (and presents an as yet unexamined subject worth at least
a small book to itself). What wants nothing to my purpose here is the
contemporaneity which is the motivating spirit of the dialogue of the
Western; for the feeling-tone of any Western is that of the time contemporary with its making, not that of the historical time in which its
action is set.

In random example, consider this remark of a sheriff to his delin-
quent deputy in Samuel Fuller's Forty Guns: "Here you are drawing
good pay in a good job and you gotta go and rob the mails—you
outta go see a head doctor!" Or note in a Scott-Boetticher movie,
Comanche Station, such expressions as: "Suit yourself" and "I should
have known!" Or, for a breathlessly Now locution, note this from
Butch Cassidy and the Sundance Kid: "Everybody else wears bifocals
—but I got vision!" This is as dead-center contemporary—and con-
temporaneously collegiate—as you can get, mainly because of that
flourishing of "vision," a word which dropped out of intellectual vogue
several years ago, but which is presently used a lot by advertising men
and by scriptwriters of youth films (which is what this one essentially

is). The film also offers less pretentious anachronisms like: "He'd better not louse it up." To the audience for Westerns this sort of lingo is not only acceptable but congenial; for no small part of the life and fun of the Western is in the curious currency and charge of its dialogue. Nor is there a better guideline to the merits and flaws in general of a Western than the dialogue. *Butch Cassidy and the Sundance Kid* is indeed a vapidly arch movie; while *The Last Sunset* ranks among the best Hollywood films of the past decade. Between these two levels, there is the more workaday and perhaps even more characteristically nutty Hollywoodian wit of a line like: "Morals? She can stretch her morals like an elastic band!" I forget the title of the film this comes from, but the line may serve to evoke that sort of desperate deftness, akin to a pickpocket's, which characterized the style, over-all, of many a good low-budget Western of the fifties.

Anachronistic speech, then, is inherent to the genre, is a part of its appeal in reflecting contemporary idioms and predispositions. This is one among the various reasons why appraisals of the Western from a realistic standard have proved so blank.

Westerns as Social and Political Alternatives

by JAMES K. FOLSOM

Probably the basic objection to Western films—usually put in terms of their being an "escape" from something or other which is doubtless more worth while—is that they are untrue to the facts of American western history. With the exception of an occasional bandit biography of doubtful authenticity and a few relatively rare cinematic treatments of particular historic events (such as *They Died with Their Boots On,* a romanticized version of the defeat of General Custer by Sitting Bull, or the various anachronistic "true" accounts of the notorious gun battle at the O. K. corral in Tombstone, Arizona), Western history is notable in Westerns primarily because of its absence. Moreover, what meager historic content there may be in Westerns tends to be generalized as, for example, in *The Sea of Grass,* which is about the conflict between cattlemen and homesteaders in general rather than in some particular range war, or as in *High Noon,* where the sheriff and his outlaw opponents fight to the death in a world carefully isolated from any particular place.

This objection may perhaps seem less compelling if one remembers that the world of the Western film is true to a certain historic feeling, if not to particular historic facts. The Western mirrors a persistent nagging doubt in American life about whether the choice which America made to become a great, capitalist, industrial power was indeed a wise one. Not surprisingly, objections to modern American life have often taken the form of myths about alternative American destinies, destinies which at least for artistic purposes Americans like to think they positively chose against. The Western, therefore, is not so much true to the facts of American western history as a mirror image of modern

Editor's title. From James K. Folsom, "'Western' Themes and Western Films," Western American Literature, II (Fall 1967), pp. 196–98. Reprinted by permission of the author.

American life, in which the virtuous Westerner, representative of an older and different order, is contrasted with a morally inferior modern —and often Eastern—world. To say, as many critics have, that Westerns are "nostalgic" is to miss the point. They do not so much yearn for an older and simpler life as attempt to set up an alternate standard of values to the often shabby ones of modern finance capitalism. Whether these values are in fact "true" of Western life is relatively unimportant; they are "true" only insofar as they form a hypothetical, self-consistent set of values opposed to modern American life.

The trick is by no means limited to Westerns. Any reader in eighteenth-century primitivism finds a very similar kind of thing, where the Noble Savage is no relation at all to the Indian or South Sea Islander whom he allegedly depicts, but a representative of a standard of values opposed to the conventional values of eighteenth-century society. In American life another alternate myth—which has striking similarities in many ways to the myth of the romantic West—is the myth of the Romantic South, usually conceived, as in *Gone with the Wind*, as representative of a set of idyllic virtues opposed to the shabby, money-grubbing, commercial morality of the North.[1] Examples could be multiplied indefinitely, but hopefully the point is clear; whatever "realism" there may be in Westerns is not to be found in the faithful reproduction of the facts of Western history but in the implied values of modern society against which Western values stand in contrast.

The contrast is often implicit, and often, it should be added, rather silly and rather heavy-handed. I remember distinctly a film biography of "Buffalo Bill" Cody which I saw as a child (and which, parenthetically, had absolutely nothing in common with the historic Buffalo Bill but the name of its hero) in which his wife, who did not like the hardships and deprivations of life in the West, took herself and their young son off to a life of ease in the East. There the boy caught diphtheria and died. Buffalo Bill carefully—if inexactly—explained to his contrite wife that diphtheria was a disease of civilization, the implication clearly being that in the West life is more "healthy."

The scene itself is ludicrous, but our objection is not so much to the metaphor—after all, Camus uses something very similar in *La Peste* —as to the clumsily didactic way in which it is presented. The end of the motion picture *Shane*, where Shane rides away from the grubby town in which the action of the film has taken place, is a more satisfactory statement of a very similar theme, as is the concluding visual metaphor of *High Noon*, where the sheriff contemptuously drops his

[1] For a more thorough comparison of the Western with the "golden myth of the ante-bellum South," see David B. Davis, "Ten-Gallon Hero," *American Quarterly*, VI (Summer, 1954), 112f.

badge in the street of the town which, though he has defended, he has found not worth defending. Perhaps best of all is the masterly interplay of ironies in *One-Eyed Jacks,* in which a bandit who has gained his freedom by betraying a friend significantly turns up later as the sheriff of an ostentatiously upright community. "You're a one-eyed jack in this town," the friend whom he has betrayed tells him, "but I see the other side of your face."

Western films, then, like Western novels, often represent a philosophical and, on occasion, political point of view which is at the very least profoundly suspicious of the development of modern American democracy.

Puritanism Revisited: An Analysis of the Contemporary Screen-Image Western

by PETER HOMANS

PRINCIPALS AND ACTION

The action of the screen-image western takes place in three phases: the opening, the action, and closing phases; or, everything before the fight, the fight, and everything after the fight.

The opening phase first of all introduces us to the story's setting, to the supporting types (through their roles) and principals. In doing so, however, it not only supplies us with information, but also provides the very important illusion that we are to see for the first time something which we know, in the back of our heads, we have seen many times before. It is important to believe that we are not idiots, watching the same story night after night.

Secondly, the opening phase prepares us for the action by delineating the hero. He is, first of all, a transcendent figure, originating beyond the town. Classically, he rides into town from nowhere; even if he is the marshal, his identity is in some way dissociated from the people he must save. We know nothing of any past activities, relationships, future plans, or ambitions. Indeed, the hero is himself often quite ambiguous about these. There are no friends, relatives, family, mistresses—not even a dog or cat—with the exception of the horse, and this too is a strangely formal relationship.

His appearance further supports this image. In the pre-action phase the hero sets forth a contrived indolence, barely distinguishable from sloth. Lax to the point of laziness, there appears to be nothing directional or purposeful about him. Take that hat, for instance: it sits

From Studies in Public Community, *no. 3 (Summer 1961), pp. 73–84. Reprinted by permission of the author.*

exactly where it was placed—no effort has been made to align it. His horse is tied to whatever happens to protrude from the ground—and remains tied, although little more than a lazy nod would free it. Clothes and gunbelt also betray the absence of any effort towards arrangement and order. With feet propped up on the hitching rail, frame balanced on a chair or stool tilted back on its two rear legs, hat pushed slightly over the eyes, hands clasped over the buckle of his gunbelt, the hero is a study in contrived indolence.

I have used the word "contrived" to indicate another quality—that of discipline and control—which remains latent, being obscured by apparent laxity. His indolence is merely superficial, and serves to protect and undergird the deeper elements of control which will appear in the action phase. Now he has time on his hands; but he knows his time is coming, and so do we.

The hero's coupling of laxity and control is seen in those recurrent primary images which are ordinarily referred to simply as "typical scenes." With woman there is no desire or attraction. He appears somewhat bored with the whole business, as if it were in the line of duty. He never blushes, or betrays any enthusiasm; he never rages or raves over a woman. His monosyllabic stammer and brevity of speech clearly indicate an intended indifference. In the drinking scenes we are likely to see him equipped with the traditional shotglass and bottle. The latter becomes his personal property, and therefore he is never questioned as to how many drinks he has taken. We rarely see him pay for more than one. While drinking he usually stares gloomily at the floor, or at all the other gloomy people who are staring gloomily at each other. He gulps his drink, rarely enjoys it, and it impatient to be off, on his way, hurrying to a place we are never told about. In the gambling scenes his poker face is to cards what his gloomy stare was to drink—a mask serving to veil any inner feelings of greed, enthusiasm, fear, or apprehension. We note, however, that he always wins, or else refuses to play. Similarly, he is utterly unimpressed and indifferent to money, regardless of its quantity or source, although the unguarded bank is always just around the corner.

The action phase opens with the threat of evil, and extends up to its destruction at the hands of the hero. Although evil is most often referred to as the "villain" or "bad guy" or "heavy," I prefer the terms "evil one" or "adversary."

Of the many hundreds of seemingly different versions, each is unshaven, darkly clothed, and from the west. Little is known about him. We are not told of his origins, his relationships, habits, or customs. Like the hero, he is from beyond the town, rather than identified with the interests, problems, and resources which characterize it. All details of his personal life are withheld. We can only be sure that the evil one unhesitatingly involves himself in the following activities: gambling, drink, the accumulation of money, lust and violence. They are his vocation; with respect to these, he is a professional man. It should be noted, however, that he is inclined to cheat at cards, get drunk, lust after women who do not return the compliment, rob banks, and finally, to shooting people he does not care for, especially heroes.

The impact of this evil on the town is electric, as though a switch had been thrown, suddenly animating it with vitality, purpose, and direction. Indeed, it is evil, rather than good, which actually gives meaning to the lives of these people—his presence elicits commitment to a cause. The townsfolk now share a new identity: they are "those who are threatened by the evil one." Unified by a common threat, the town loses its desolate, aimless quality. It becomes busy. Some hasten to protect others; some to protect themselves; some run for help; some comment fearfully. Nevertheless, they all know (as do we) that they are of themselves ultimately powerless to meet this evil. What is required is the hero—a transcendent power originating from beyond the town.

Notice what has happened to this power. Gone are the indolence, laxity, and lack of intention. Now he is infused with vitality, direction, and seriousness. Before, the most trivial item might have caught his attention; now, every prior loyalty and concern are thoroughly excluded—he drops everything—in order that he may confront with passion and single-mindedness this ultimate threat. Once this radical shift has been accomplished, the hero (and audience) are ready for the final conflict—the central part of the action phase, the climax of the story.

While the fight can take many forms (fist-fight, fight with knives, whips, etc.—even a scowling match in which the hero successfully glares down the evil one), the classical and most popular form is the encounter with six-guns. It is a built-up and drawn-out affair, always allowing enough time for an audience to gather. The two men must adhere to an elaborate and well-defined casuistry as to who draws first, when it is proper to draw, when it is not, etc. The climax also reflects much of the craft of gunplay, of which both hero and evil one are the skilled artisans (cross-draw versus side-draw, fanning versus thumbing, whether two guns are really better than one, etc.). While these issues are certainly not the main concern of the action, the prominence given them by the story as a whole tends to prolong the climax.

Although the hero's presence usually makes the fight possible—i.e., he insists on obstructing the evil one in some way—it is the latter who invariably attacks first. Were the hero ever to draw first, the story would no longer be a western. Regardless of the issues involved, or of the moral responsibility for what is to follow, the hero's final, victorious shot is always provoked by the evil one. With the destruction of the evil one, the action phase is completed.

In the closing phase the town and its hero return to their pre-action ways. The electric quality of alarm and the sense of purpose and direction recede. People come out of hiding to acclaim their hero and enjoy his victory. He too returns to his pre-action mode of indolence and laxity. At such a moment he is likely to become immediately absorbed in some unimportant detail (like blowing the smoke from his gun), indicating for all to see that he has survived the crisis and is once again his old self.

One more event must take place, however, before the story can conclude. The hero must renounce any further involvement with the town which his victory may have suggested. In some way the town offers him the opportunity to identify with it, to settle down. Traditionally, this means marrying the schoolmarm and settling down. The hero always refuses. He cannot identify himself with the situation he has saved. He forfeits any opportunity to renounce his "beyond the town" origin and destiny. When this forfeiture has been made clear, when both savior and saved realize that it cannot be abrogated, then the story is over.

ANALYSIS

The western is, as most people by this time are willing to acknowledge, a popular myth. And by myth I mean three things. First of all, it is a story whose basic patterns of character, plot, and detail are repeated again and again, and can be so recognized. Secondly, the story embodies and sets forth certain meanings about what is good and bad, right and wrong—meanings regarded as important by those who view and participate in the myth. And thirdly, some of these meanings are veiled by the story,[1] so that one can affirm them without overtly acknowledging them. Some part of the story (or all of it, perhaps) serves to conceal something from the participant—i.e., there is an unacknowledged aspect to the story. There is, therefore, an embarrassing question which never occurs to those in the sway of the myth—the posing of which is precisely the critic's most important task.

The meanings which the western sets forth center upon the problem of good and evil. Evil, according to the myth, is the failure to resist temptation. It is loss of control. Goodness lies in the power and willingness to resist temptation. It is the ability to remain in the presence of temptation and yet remain in control of one's desire. Five activities make up the well-known content of temptation: drinking, gambling, money, sex, and violence.

---

[1] This point is drawn from DeRougemont's analysis of the myth of Tristan and Isolde. See Denis DeRougemont, *Love in the Western World*. New York: Pantheon Press, 1956.

Whenever any one of these activities appears it should be seen as a self-contained temptation episode.[2] Such an episode first of all presents an object of temptation which can be indulged, should the hero so choose; and secondly, it sets forth the hero in such a way that he can indulge the temptation in a preliminary way without becoming absorbed in it—i.e., without losing control. And, of course, it sets forth the evil one in precisely the opposite way.

In the drinking scenes the hero possesses not one drink, but a whole bottle—i.e., he has at his disposal the opportunity for unlimited indulgence and its consequent loss of self-control. Gambling is a situation over which one has rather limited control—you can lose; but the hero does not lose. He wins, thereby remaining in control (cheating simply signifies the failure to acknowledge loss of control). Wealth is not seized although it is available to him through the unguarded bank; and both good and bad girl seek out the hero in their various ways, but to no avail—he remains a hero. However, each temptation is presented in its peculiar way in order to set forth hero and evil one in their respective functions.

The temptation to do violence is more problematic, so much more so that the climax is given over to its solution. Furthermore, in the climax we find the key to the meaning of the myth as a whole—i.e., it can tell us why each type appears as he does, why the temptation episodes have their unique shape, and why certain fundamental images recur as they do.

We perceive in the evil one a terrible power, one which cannot be overcome by the ordinary resources of the town. However, he has acquired this power at great price: he has forfeited that very control and resistance which sustains and makes the hero what he is. The evil one represents, therefore, not temptation, so much as "temptation-unhesitatingly-given-into." He is the embodiment of the failure to resist temptation; he is the failure of denial. This is the real meaning of evil in the myth of the western, and it is this which makes the evil one truly evil. Because of this he threatens the hero's resistance (and that of the townsfolk, as well, although indirectly): each taunt and baiting gesture is a lure to the foreiture of control. This temptation the hero cannot handle with the usual methods of restraint, control, and the refusal to become absorbed; and it leads to a temptation which the hero cannot afford to resist: the temptation to destroy temptation.

The evil one's dark appearance is related to this threat. It tells us two things. First, that to lose control and forfeit resistance is (according to the story) a kind of living death, for black signifies death. In

[2] I am not suggesting that every western has all of these temptations, or that they appear in any given order. The subject of analysis is the representative version—not any particular version or set of versions. Thus any particular western might deal with any one, or a number of such temptations.

terms of the moral instruction of the story, and speaking metaphorically, we know that the evil one has "lost his life." But his black appearance also tells us that, speaking quite literally, this man will die —because of what he is, he must and will be executed. We are therefore both instructed and reassured.

The embarrassing question can now be posed: why must the hero wait to be attacked, why must he refrain from drawing first? Why does he not take his opponent from behind, while he is carousing, or while he is asleep? Anyone in the power of the myth would reply that the gunfight takes place the way it does because this is the way westerns are; it's natural; this is the way it's always done—or, in the language of the myth itself, it was self-defense. But if one moves beyond the grasp of the myth, if one is no longer loyal to its rules and values, the gunfight is never inevitable. The circumstances which force the hero into this situation are contrived in order to make the violent destruction of the evil one appear just and virtuous. These cirumstances have their origin in the inner, veiled need to which the story is addressed. This process, whereby desire is at once indulged and veiled I call the "inner dynamic." It is the key to the western, explaining not only the climax of the story, but everything else uniquely characteristic of it. What is required is that temptation be indulged while providing the appearance of having been resisted.

Each of the minor temptation episodes—the typical scenes setting forth hero and evil one as each encounters drink, cards, money, and sex—takes its unique shape from this need. Each is a climaxless western in itself, a play within a play in which temptation is faced and defeated, not by violent destruction, as in the climax, but by inner, willed control. Or reversing the relationship, we may say that in the gunfight we have writ large something which takes place again and again throughout the story. It is precisely for this reason that no western has or needs to have all these episodes. Therefore westerns can and do depart radically from the composite picture described earlier. We are so familiar with each kind of temptation, and each so reinforces the others that extraordinary deletions and variations can occur without our losing touch with the central meanings.

The inner dynamic affects the supporting types as well. The derelict professional is derelict, and the nonviolent easterner is weak, precisely because they have failed to resist temptation in the manner characteristic of the hero. Their moderate, controlled indulgence of the various temptations does not conform to the total resistance of the hero. Consequently they must be portrayed as derelict, weak and deficient men, contrasting unfavorably with the hero's virtue. In this sense they have more in common with the evil one.

Because these two types both originate in the east, they have something in common with the good girl. We note that everything eastern in the western is considered weak, emotional, and feminine (family life, intellectual life, domestic life, professional life). Only by becoming westernized can the east be redeemed. The western, therefore, is more a myth about the east than it is about the west: it is a secret and bitter parody of eastern ways. This is all the more interesting, since it was originally written in the east, by easterners, for eastern reading. It really has very little to do with the west.

Woman is split in the western to correspond to the splitting of man into hero and evil one. Primarily, however, the double feminine image permits the hero some gratification of desire while making a stalemate ultimately necessary. To get the good girl, the story instructs us, our hero would have to become like those despicable easterners; to get the bad girl, he would have to emulate the evil one. In such a dilemma a ride into the sunset is not such a bad solution after all.

The attendant sets forth the inner dynamic by being infinitely close to the action (temptations) while never becoming at all involved in it. It is his task to provide the instruments of temptation (drink, money, cards, guns) while never indulging them himself. He is at once closer to temptation than any other type, and yet more removed than any other type.

The boys function to facilitate the action without becoming involved in it. Without them hero and adversary might find other ways to settle their differences. The boys serve to remind them of their obligations to each other and the story as a whole, thereby structuring the myth more firmly. While they are around nothing less than the traditional gunfight will do. On the other hand, because they never participate in the action, but only coerce and reinforce it, they are thoroughly resistant to this temptation as well.

In summary, then: the western is a myth in which evil appears as a series of temptations to be resisted by the hero—most of which he succeeds in avoiding through inner control. When faced with the embodiment of these temptations, his mode of control changes, and he destroys the threat. But the story is so structured that the reponsibility for this act falls upon the adversary, permitting the hero to destroy while appearing to save. Types and details, as well as narrative, take their shape from this inner dynamic, which must therefore be understood as the basic organizing and interpretive principle for the myth as a whole.

CULTURAL IMPLICATIONS

The western, I believe, bears a significant relationship—both dynamic and historical—to a cultural force which, for lack of a better word, I would call "puritanism." Here I simply refer to a particular normative image of man's inner life in which it is the proper task of the will to rule, control, and contain the spontaneous, vital aspects of life. For the puritan there is little interpenetration between will and feeling, will and imagination. The will dominates rather than participates in the feelings and imagination.

Whenever vitality becomes too pressing, and the dominion of the will becomes threatened, the self must find some other mode of control. In such a situation the puritan will seek, usually unknowingly, any situation which will permit him to express vitality while at the same time appearing to control and resist it. The western provides just this opportunity, for, as we have seen, the entire myth is shaped by the inner dynamic of apparent control and veiled expression. Indeed, in the gunfight (and to a lesser extent in the minor temptation episodes) the hero's heightened gravity and dedicated exclusion of all other loyalties presents a study in puritan virtue, while the evil one presents nothing more nor less than the old New England protestant devil—strangely costumed, to be sure—the traditional tempter whose horrid lures never allow the good puritan a moment's peace. In the gunfight there is deliverance and redemption. Here is the real meaning of the western: a puritan morality tale in which the savior-hero redeems the community from the temptations of the devil.

The western is also related to puritanism through its strong self-critical element—i.e., it attacks, usually through parody, many aspects of traditional civilized life. Self-criticism, however, does not come easily to the puritan. Like vitality, it functions through imagination; and it too is in the service of the will. Therefore, if such criticism is to appear at all, it too must be veiled. The western assists in this difficult problem, for the story is well removed from his own locale, both geographically and physically. Because it is always a story taking place "out there," and "a long time ago," self-criticism can appear without being directly recognized as such.

It is tempting to inquire how far certain historical forms of puritanism, such as mass religious revivals, may have actually produced the western. Was it only a coincidence that the same period of 1905–1920, which saw the early emergence of the western myth, also witnessed the nationwide popularity of a Billy Sunday and an Aimee Semple McPherson? Their gospel was a radical triumph of will over feeling and vitality, through which the believer could rely wholly upon his increasingly omnipotent will for the requisite controls. And here too was the familiar inventory of vices, with its characteristic emphasis upon gambling and drinking.

Recently there has been an even more remarkable religious revival. Beginning in the early 1950's, it reached its point of greatest intensity in 1955. Here the gentle willfulness of the Graham gospel, and the more subtle (but equally hortatory) "save-yourself" of the Peale contingent permitted many respectable people to go to church and become interested in religion, without actually knowing why. However, like its earlier counterpart, this was not so much a religious movement as it was a renewed attack of the will upon the life of feeling and vitality.

Presently, however, the religious revival has subsided, but the western remains almost as popular as ever. This could mean one of two things. On the one hand, the many changes which the western is presently undergoing—in its narrative, its types, and in its recurrent, primary images—could indicate that the religious recession has permitted the myth to be altered radically, such that it is on the way to becoming something entirely different. On the other hand, should such changes remain responsible to and be contained by the classical version, it could be that our puritanism is simply being expressed through nonreligious sources: most notably through the social sciences (indeed, in the sociologist's and psychologist's denunciation of the violence, historical inaccuracies, etc. in the western, do we not hear echoes of the puritan hero himself?).

Savior in the Saddle:
The Sagebrush Testament
by MICHAEL T. MARSDEN

As Frederick Jackson Turner pointed out, the birth of a new land demanded the simultaneous birth of a new culture, with its roots necessarily in the past, but its blossom in the timeless experience of the ever-extending and never-ending frontier.[1] This operative truth is acted out time and again as Western after Western unfolds on movie screens across this land. It is logical, therefore, to suggest that notions of a Savior, a Messiah, would have undergone a similar transformation from the Christian Savior of almost nineteen hundred years of European cultural refinement to a Christ equipped to serve the essentially different spiritual needs of a new and separate culture. Nowhere is this transformation more clearly seen than in the Western film.

American heroes have a long tradition of serving as the Redeemer. For the Puritans, the wilderness of their "Chosen Land" was inhabited by devils, and these devils could be driven out only by the strongest and worthiest of men. If the land was to be settled, it had to be tamed and purified. It is of this challenge that the American hero, beginning with Daniel Boone, was born. And Boone's direct cultural descendant, the Western hero, became America's most permanent heroic creation, serving as Redeemer for generations of Americans.

However, it is interesting that, while criticism of the Western film has suggested the Savior-like nature of the Western hero, no extended treatment has been given to the divine, Savior-like qualities of this American creation. Harry Schein, for example, in an article entitled

[1] *The Turner Thesis Concerning the Role of the Frontier in American History,* edited by George Rogers Taylor. Boston: D.C. Heath and Co., 1956.

"The Olympian Cowboy," suggests that in the western landscape one can discern "an Olympian landscape model, the Rocky Mountains— saturated with divine morality." [2] A little later in that same article he suggests that Shane is "an American saint . . . and sits at God's right hand." [3] But these suggestions are never explored. Martin Nussbaum, in his article "The 'Adult Western' As An American Art Form," argues that the gun is a symbol of divine intervention into the American landscape, but he never entertains the implications of this regarding the nature of the Western hero.[4]

It is the purpose of this study to establish several of the religious parallels that abound in Western film, and then to crystallize them into a statement regarding the religious nature of the Western hero. The West of the American imagination is the landscape for this study, not the West as it was, but the West, as John Ford would say, as it should have been.

It is practically a commonplace for people to refer to the Western gunfighter-hero as an American parallel to the medieval knight.[5] While such mediations seem appropriate and stimulate interest, there is a very real danger that they will cloud the issue of the particular and unique nature of the American Western hero; he is an American god, who in the name of a divinely ordered civilization carries a Colt .45. As Gary Cooper succinctly put it, the five bullets in the cylinder were for law and order, and the one in the chamber was for justice. The Western formula clearly implies that the Messiah of the New Testament was unacceptable to a land of savagery, harsh landscape, and purple sunsets. The West needed a Christ who could survive the Great American Desert, and for much longer than forty days and who could show himself equal to the American challenge, whether real or imagined. And this Savior would have to be equal to the wishes and dreams of a suffering people who wished to be delivered from the concretized evil that plagued their lives. The people longed for a Christ who would ride in, deal effectively with evil, and dispense justice with a finality that would make the angels envious and a skill that John Cawelti, in his book *The Six-Gun Mystique* likens to that of a surgeon.[6] But this Western Savior must, of necessity, bring with him all the trappings of a just and, at times, wrathful God, as in the Old Testament. He could not

[2] Harry Shein, "The Olympian Cowboy." *American Scholar*, Vol. 24 (Summer, 1955), 317.

[3] Shein, p. 319.

[4] Martin Nussbaum, "The 'Adult Western' As An American Art Form." *Folklore*, Vol. 70 (September, 1959), 464.

[5] See, for example, Joseph J. Waldmeir, "The Cowboy, The Knight, and Popular Taste." Southern Folklore Quarterly, XXII:3 (September, 1958), 113–120.

[6] John G. Cawelti, *The Six-Gun Mystique*. Bowling Green, Ohio: Bowling Green State University Popular Press, 1970, p. 59.

ent, but must be, rather, a Christ who has been modified, changed
by contact with the Western experience. The lawlessness of the frontier required a strong sense of divine justice untempered with mercy.
The coming of the Western hero is a kind of Second Coming of Christ,
but this time he wears the garb of the gunfighter, the only Savior the
sagebrush, the wilderness, and the pure savagery of the West can
accept.

"A JUST GOD AND A SAVIOR, THERE IS NONE BESIDES
ME."—*Isaiah* 45:21

The West of the American imagination needed a clean, swift, sure
and final justice in a lawless land infested by outlaws, Indians, and a
a hostile and threatening environment. The Western film mythology,
from the very beginnings of film history, combined the best myths
available to forge a viable and lasting mythology which, until recently
with the release of anti-Westerns such as *Bad Company* (1972), *Soldier Blue* (1970), and *Dirty Little Billy* (1972), has remained intact,
and would appear to be able to weather even the tumultuous filmic
assaults being waged against it during the last decade.

Finally, in dealing with the nature of the Western hero, it seems
fruitful to view him as a coming together of certain elements from the
Old and the New Testaments, and to see through him the creation of
a Sagebrush Testament with its own ethos.

"BEHOLD THE DAYS COME, SAITH THE LORD, AND I
WILL RAISE UP TO DAVID A JUST BRANCH; AND A KING
SHALL REIGN, AND SHALL BE WISE; AND SHALL EXE-
CUTE A JUDGMENT AND JUSTICE IN THE EARTH."
—*Jeremiah* 23:5

In 1916 William S. Hart starred in and directed an allegorical Western entitled *Hell's Hinges*. Hart plays the role of Blaze Tracy, who, as
one title says, represents a two-gun "embodiment of the best and the
worst in the early west." As the film opens he embodies primarily the
worst. We find him in league with Silk Miller, owner of the local
saloon, aptly named "The Palace of Joy." The town is awaiting the
arrival of a rather weak and selfish young parson who has been sent
by his Bishop to establish a Church in the wilderness and prove himself as a clergyman. God does not, however, abide in Hell's Hinges,
a truth which the inexperienced parson and his lovely sister, Faith,
must soon painfully face.

As Tracy first gazes at Faith, it is "One who is evil, looking for the
first time on what is good." Later, Tracy, who was expected by the

corrupt townspeople to take part in the elimination of the parson from Hell's Hinges, stands up for the clergyman and his congregation as they hold their first church service in a local barn. The dance-hall girls, rabble-rousers, and other nonbelievers decide to break up the ceremony by holding a dance on the same premises. But Blaze Tracy's two guns convince them to allow the Sunday service to continue.

When the parson's sister, Faith, attempts to "convert" Blaze, he utters: "I reckon God ain't wantin' me much ma'am, but when I look at you, I feel I've been ridin' the wrong trail." He seeks out religion because Faith holds stock in it, and there must therefore be some value in it. When the parson is lured into the lead dancehall girl's boudoir, plied with drink, and seduced, it is Blaze who tells a parable to the bewildered good townspeople, who are now a leaderless flock. He tells them, in a Christ-like and kindly New Testament manner, about Arizona, a renowned cowboy roper who set off to rope a calf, but the rope failed him. Thus, he says, it was the instrument they counted on that failed them, not their faith.

The evil townspeople are so depraved that they conspire to burn down the newly erected church. So effective have they been in destroying the parson that he is first in line with a willing hand and a lighted torch. But, before he can act, he is killed by the remaining good people who will shed blood to protect their church. After considerable bloodshed, and while Blaze is away on an errand of mercy, the church is burned down. The few remaining good people are literally sent into the desert, to await the return of the Savior who will seek revenge for the destruction of the church and the death of the parson. Blaze, living up to his first name, guns down Silk Miller and turns the whole town into a living inferno. He gives Hell's Hinges a "crown of fire," and forcefully damns it to eternity. In short, Faith is helpless in the West unless she has two blazing guns to defend her. The Western Savior needs the confrontation with civilization (formal religion) to tame him, but he can easily arrive at heroic stature because of his essential goodness.

In *Hell's Hinges* there is the obvious, but nonetheless effective illustration of the blending of certain divine qualities from the Old and New Testament to form a kind of Sagebrush Testament, which must of necessity result in the forging of a new Savior, who is of the sagebrush, but also superior to it.

The 1931 film *Cimarron,* the only Western ever to receive the Oscar for Best Picture, contains another powerful illustration of the essential transformation of Christianity through the American imagination in the Western Yancey Cravat (Richard Dix) is an incurable wanderer who finds himself in Oklahoma as a consequence of the land rush into the Indian territory opened for settlement. In turn, he becomes a poet, gunfighter, lawyer, and editor, and is successful at each. Being a leading citizen, he is bound to defend the forces of civilization over the forces of the lawless frontier. During one scene, in order to bring religion to the frontier, he himself preaches a sermon. He pulls out a Bible from his back pocket, and as he draws it forward it crosses the butt of his holstered gun as a warning to all who would attempt to usurp the forces of civilization. The saloon is his church, and instead of a crucifix in the background, there is the traditional saloon nude. Christ has come to the frontier, but he wears a different garb and follows a new ethos, a modified ethos that was born of the confrontation with the land and savagery. In the middle of his sermon, Yancey Cravat uses his free hand to draw his six-gun and shoot down several unruly cowboys who are disrupting his preaching!

The Savior-like nature of the Western hero is nowhere more clearly manifested than in George Stevens' masterful *Shane* (1953). Alan Ladd at the beginning of the film moves slowly down the Grand Teton Mountains from the West. He is the new Christ, the frontier Christ, coming down from a Western Olympus to help the cause of the farmers against the ranchers. We see Shane through the eyes of America's future, young Joey Starrett, through whom the tradition Shane represents will be handed down. Shane is the pearl-handled-gun-toting Messiah who *can* save the endangered land from the forces of lawlessness. It is not by accident that Joey's parents are named Joe and Marion, standing in wait for the Messiah-son who will deliver them. The suggestion by some critics that Joey may well be dreaming the entire story seems to work well here. For Shane is what Joey wants to become and what Joe and Marion want their son to become. Shane brings with him all the trappings of a wrathful God out of the Old Testament—omniscience, swift judgment/justice, and an anger born of injustice. But that "wrath" is only hinted at in the early parts of the film as some dangerous undercurrent in the man. As the film opens, he has attempted to hang up his guns, to live peacefully, kindly, and gently. But experience proves that evil must be dealt with directly, swiftly, and surely.

The Devil is personified in this film by the hired gunman, Jack Wilson (Jack Palance), who shoots down an innocent farmer to instill fear in the homesteaders. When the farmers are burying their murdered compatriot and are considering giving up the land, it is Shane who, in the middle of a barren cemetery with the flimsy, false-fronted town to his back, reminds them about what is at stake in this epic struggle. He preaches his sermon on the mount effectively, and they depart reassured, determined, and unified. Shane, however, by unwillingly but obediently accepting the burden of the homesteaders, sacrifices his right to the good life. He was sent from the mountain to perform a task of salvation, and although he struggles mightily with his fate and wishes it were otherwise, he does not, in his moment of truth, hesitate to shoulder the burden of being a savior. He, finally, plays the hand he has been dealt.

But before he sacrifices himself he instructs Joey in the use of the gun. Martin Nussbaum has correctly observed that the gun is really a "deus ex machina" in the Western.[7] It is the "word" of the West, and must be understood and used correctly. The temptation is to limit one's interpretation of the gun to sexual suggestions, which are indeed clearly there in *Shane* as in other Westerns. Marion, for example, is both fascinated by the power Shane possesses through the gun, and afraid of it. The Western hero must use the gun deliberately and sparingly so that, in the words of Judd in *Ride The High Country* (1962), he can "enter his house justified." Shane tells Marion and Joey that it is not the gun that is evil, but rather the way in which it is used. It is only a tool, he explains, neither good nor bad in itself. Shane leaves Joey instructed. And when Joey runs to town after Shane, watches over his hero, and finally warns him of the danger, he is found tested and true.

After the showdown, Shane, who incidentally has been wounded in the left side, and who is about to ride off into the mountains again, stops and lays his hand upon the head of young Joey, as if to consecrate him for the task ahead.[8] But this Messiah needs only one apostle, not twelve. For the Christianity of the American imagination, of the American Desert, is an individualistic one.

From *Shane* to the cynical "Dollars" films of the 1960's is a long leap, but the image of the Savior clings even to Eastwood's portrayal of the self-interested yet fated Messiah of a deserving few. In *Fistfull of Dollars* (1964—American release 1967), Eastwood rides into a Southwestern town on a mule. He is shot at, poked fun at, and swings from a crosslike beam. The whole scene suggests a Palm Sunday in reverse. As a consequence of doing battle with the evil forces in the town, he receives a terrible beating including, appropriately, a wound on the hand. He seeks sanctuary in a coffin, and is reborn again to fight evil, seeming to be invulnerable to shots in the heart by wearing an armor breastplate. In a touching sequence, suggestive of the Holy Family's flight from Bethlehem to the desert, Eastwood frees a captive mother, her helpless husband, and their young son and sends them off into the desert to seek refuge. Eastwood, "the man with no name," like

---

[7] Nussbaum, p. 464.

[8] Joey was, of course, played by Brandon de Wilde, who later starred in *Hud* as the teen-age nephew of Hud who turned away in disgust from all that he represented. Brandon de Wilde died at the age of thirty-three, as did, in 1973, Carl B. Bradley, who played the Marlboro cowboy in a national advertising campaign. The author does not wish to suggest anything more than that such curiosities in light of the Christ parallels prove to be interesting musings for the imaginative.

the heroes of American-made Westerns, brings justice (and mercy) to this evil-ridden society through violence.

Eastwood returned in 1973 as the "no name" character in a Western of his own creation, *High Plains Drifter,* in which he eschews traditional religion because it did not intervene when the town had bull-whipped the Marshal to death in its streets. He comes to the town to execute an elaborate but just revenge upon its inhabitants. While pushing aside the parson who speaks empty Christians platitudes, "No Name" dispenses justice with an appropriateness that defies parallels. The cowardly townsfolk are, for example, led to believe they can be made courageous under his leadership. He, however, trains them and leaves them, taking with him their supposed courage. Called a Guardian Angel by some, the Devil by others, he turns out to be their judge and, like God, allows men to work out their own destinies, trapping and destroying themselves. As a final insult, he has them paint the whole town red, suggesting the crown of fire so memorable from *Hell's Hinges,* and he even paints "Hell" over the town's name on the sign at the edge of the town.

Alejandro Jodorowsky, a South American director, has successfully employed the convention of the Sagebrush Savior in his ultraviolent and enigmatic film, *El Topo* (1971). El Topo rides into the desert with his son, abandons him to his own devices, and seeks adventure in the Great Desert. After numerous violent experiences, he is shot by a woman companion, left for dead, and rescued by a tribe of cave-dwelling mutants who are kept in underground confinement by the neighboring townspeople. While living among these strange people, he becomes a kind of pacifist Savior and eventually leads them to freedom from their confinement. But when they rush en masse into the Mexican village, they are promptly slaughtered by the forces of evil. El Topo, seeing the slaughter, grabs a rifle and, declaring in turn that he is Justice and then God, consecrates the bullets with his words. He becomes the personification of violence, seemingly invulnerable to bullets himself. The film ends in a holocaust as El Topo destroys the villains with his rifle and then immolates himself, Buddhist monk fashion, in the middle of the main street, etching forever in the minds of the viewers the inevitability of justice through violence.

Films such as *El Topo* serve as illustrations of the viability of the Savior convention, as the Western is adapted to the cultural needs of other nations which seek to develop it as a unique folk-pop art within their own cultural contexts and thus re-examine it in that milieu.

Criticism of the Western film must take into account the transformation of a Christian mythology as much as the transformation of other cultural traditions. The Western hero cannot simply be a Christ transported out of the New Testament anymore than he can be a slightly altered medieval knight. For in the American imagination, the New

Testament message of love and mercy does not provide solutions any more than the American judicial system does. The answer lies in divine intervention, through a hero who combines the most useful qualities of the Old Testament God and the New Testament Christ, to create a Sagebrush Savior who is kind, yet strong; who is just, yet firm. This hero is the only hero the Western can abide by in a wilderness which is ever ready to snuff out civilization as it weakly struggles to exist in flimsy wooden churches, schools, and town halls, strung out like cross-bearing telephone poles against the ever-widening horizon. The hero must be suprahuman, and he must, above all, be invulnerable to the human weaknesses shared by those whom he must defend and protect. If he is to be the answer to the dreams and prayers of the troubled, he must ride tall, shoot straight, and remain eternally vigilant for the causes of right.

But in order to create the needed hero the Western had to borrow from numerous sources to form the truly viable and invulnerable Savior who rides in, provides a definite and final solution to the problem, and rides out as inevitably and often as our psyches dictate. He, like the Christian Messiah, must always be with us, ever ready to sweep down on the evil towns and destroy them so they can be rebuilt to house families and civilization and the dreams of men. He may exist only in the American imagination, but he has the will of a people to give him strength and their hearts to give him immortality.

The author would like to express his debt of appreciation to Jack Nachbar for many hours of stimulating conversation on the topic of Western films, and for providing the catalystic conception that the Western hero was more of the Old Testament than the New Testament.

THE
•○❧ CONTEMPORARY ❧○•
WESTERN

Riding Shotgun:
The Scattered Formula in
Contemporary Western Movies
by JACK NACHBAR

In John Ford's 1946 film, *My Darling Clementine,* the motives for
the gunfight at the OK corral are very clear—the Clantons have murdered two Earp brothers. As the head of the Earp family, and as marshal of Tombstone, Wyatt Earp (Henry Fonda) has both the right and
the duty to kill the Clantons. It is no surprise, then, that after the famous battle, Earp is recognized as the hero of the community and will
soon be rewarded by wedding the lovely maiden from the East, Clementine Carter.

Twenty-one years after *My Darling Clementine* Wyatt again faced

From The Film Journal, *vol. 2, no. 3 (September 1973). This article
appeared in slightly different form therein. Reprinted by permission of*
The Film Journal.

the Clanton guns at the OK corral in John Sturges' *Hour of the Gun.*
This time, however, things turned out differently. After the shoot-out,
Earp (James Garner) is told that he acted in violation of the law and
is arrested, and tried. Later, as in Ford's film, two of Earp's brothers
are ambushed and Wyatt goes after the killers. "He wants them because the law says to take them," Doc Holiday (Jason Robards) says
idealistically of Earp. But each time Earp confronts a killer, he taunts
him into a gunfight and kills him. In 1967, Wyatt Earp is no longer
a defender of the law; he contemptuously hides under the law to satisfy his near-psychotic lust for violent revenge. Obviously between
1946 and 1967 there were some important changes in the legend of
Wyatt Earp. The same may be said of the entire Western formula. Like
terrified shotgun riders on a Wells Fargo stage blasting away at shad-
ows, the creators of contemporary Western movies are nervously aim-
ing their genre in several directions at once. And like pellets from that
shotgun, the Western formula is spreading out into a wide and confusing pattern.

According to John Cawelti, the "formula" or standard plot structure
of a Western is centered in an "epic moment" of confrontation between the pioneer and the wilderness.[1] The pioneer, civilized, progressive, and orderly, pits himself against the American landscape, a savage
land full of the forces of chaos—violent outlaws and bloodthirsty
Indians. At the precise moment of the Western plot, two forces are in
a standoff. But since the audience knows they are part of the civilization that finally conquered the wilderness, it is understood that the
town, or the ranch, or the homestead is the sympathetic party in the
confrontation.

Standing between civilization and the wilderness is the Western
hero. The hero is civilized in that usually his life is patterned after a
gentlemanly code.[2] He, for example, never draws first, and never uses
an unfair weapon in a hand-to-hand fight. However, like the forces of
chaos in the wilderness, he obtains his ends through violence, usually
with a blazing colt. This man, with a foot in each world, ultimately obtains his heroic stature by defending the tamers of the land against the
vicious forces of destruction in the wilds. The use of violence is morally
justified because the hero uses it to aid the historic progress of civilization.

This conventional formula is still recognizable in most contemporary Westerns. But oftentimes just barely so. For, as in the case of
Hour of the Gun, heroes are no longer necessarily heroic, the civilized

---

[1] John G. Cawelti, *The Six-Gun Mystique.* Bowling Green, Ohio: Bowling Green
University Popular Press, 1971.

[2] The most famous description of the Western hero and his code is Robert Warshow's "The Westerner," in *The Immediate Experience.* Garden City, N.Y.: Doubleday & Co., 1962, pp. 135–54.

no longer necessarily civilized. During the past few years, filmmakers have been remolding most of the formerly standard elements of the Western. What has emerged are four basically different types of Western movie, each with its own attitude and meaning.

The first type of contemporary Western is the completely conventional product we are all used to. The conflict between civilization and the forces of the threatening wilderness is immediately apparent. We easily recognize the hero and the violent duty that lies before him. This is the case in some of the latest films of two saddle-hardened Westerners who together account for nearly seventy years of frontier heroics—Burt Lancaster and John Wayne.

In *Valdez Is Coming* (1970), Lancaster, in the title role, begins the film as a easy-going middle-aged Mexican who makes a leisurely living riding shotgun for a stagecoach line. But behind the lazy greaser countenance are tough years as a well-known American army scout and buffalo hunter. Aroused when he accidently shoots an innocent man and later is beaten horribly when he tries to collect money for the widow, Valdez dons his old scouting clothes, and proceeds to kill off a gang of pursuers. An uncannily skillful gunman, Valdez uses an old Sharps buffalo gun to shoot men out of the saddle a full half-mile away. The picture ends with Valdez confronting the head of the gang and demanding the money for the widow. The formula is clearly followed by having Valdez come to the aid of civilization, represented by the widow. Wilderness terror is illustrated by the brutality of the gang. And Valdez's killing of more than half a dozen men is neatly justified by his never forgetting that it is all for the wife of a man innocently killed.

The second type of contemporary Western movie must dismay a veteran conventional Western star like John Wayne, for it represents a contempt and usually an ironic scorn for the traditional Westerns that Wayne so doggedly keeps on making. Robert Warshow named this form the "anti-Western" and noted that its real concern was usually, "social drama," that is, the exploitation of the Western formula to criticize modern social evils.[3] As examples Warshow cites *The Ox-Bow Incident* (1943), with its condemnation of lynching, and *High Noon* (1951) where, in an obvious analogy to the then-current McCarthy witch hunt, Gary Cooper is deserted by all of his friends and must face the killers alone. Andrew Sarris further refines Warshow's definition when he says "anti-Westerns merely use the West as an allegorical device to denounce the East."[4] To the fan of the anti-Western, Westerns are corrupt because they glorify the use of violence, just as the modern "system" is corrupt for the same reasons.

[3] Warshow, pp. 148–49.
[4] Andrew Sarris, *Confessions of a Cultist: On the Cinema 1955–1969*. New York: Simon and Schuster, 1971, p. 387.

At its best, the anti-Western's basic cynicism presents a rather interesting tension in relation to the high idealism of the traditional Western.

A serious but sly and ironic anti-Western is Martin Ritt's *Hombre* (1967). The central character in *Hombre,* John Russell (Paul Newman), has all the standard Western hero trappings. He has been raised by the Indians and his dealings with his adopted people are honorable and loyal, proving he governs his life by a code. Yet Russell feels only hatred and disgust for civilized society, and in a rejection of the hero role, refuses to lift a finger to help endangered white people. We soon see why, however. Russell boards a stagecoach with a group of passengers representing a microcosm of the society as a whole. But unlike John Ford's *Stagecoach* (1939), in which most of the passengers are shown to possess courage and nobility, *Hombre* presents a coach full of crooks and cowards. One of the passengers, Grimes, turns out to be a stage robber; another passenger, Favor, a newly appointed Indian agent, is in reality stealing the Indians' money; Favor's wife is cheating on her husband. Only Jessie, the hearty proprietress of a boarding-house, has the compassion normally seen in Western settlers. In the final scenes of the film, Russell's indifference toward the others is finally broken down by Jessie, who convinces him to try to rescue Mrs. Favor away from Grimes and his gang of cutthroats. Russell is killed, and in the final image of the film we are left with live characters who, with the exception of Jessie, don't deserve to live. Ritt thus casts doubt on the integrity of the traditional Western by concluding that aiding society is ultimately an empty, wasted and meaningless act.

There is an attempt in some recent Westerns to bridge the gap of exaggerated good and overstated evil in the Western. This type of "realistic" look at frontier life may be termed the "new-Western." Unlike the anti-Western, which uses the Western formula as a vehicle of social criticism, the new-Western dismisses the formula altogether.

Will Penny (1968) establishes its break from the formula Western in its opening scene. After a cattle drive has ended, a feud between Will (Charlton Heston) and another drover, Shorthorn, erupts into a fist-fight. True to the hero's code, Shorthorn tries to fight with his fists but Will elbows, knees and bangs away at Shorthorn with any implement he can grab. Finally, Shorthorn complains, "You ain't fightin' fair."

"You're the one that's down," says Penny. "I use my hands for work." Will concludes the discussion by smashing Shorthorn across the back of the head with a tin plate.

During its best moments *Will Penny* details the endurance and hardship of cowboy life. A man has his leg crushed in a cattle pen and there is only a moment's concern. A cattle drive ends at some railroad track that stops in the middle of nowhere and the hands simply ride off satisfied the drive is over, hoping they can get winter jobs. After

Will lands a job as a line rider at a section of the ranch four days' ride away, the owner tells him, "I don't want to hear from you till spring." And a badly wounded cowboy is saved when he stops bleeding because he nearly freezes in a wagon while his friends are inside drinking and betting on whether or not he will make it to town alive.

Monte Walsh (1970), like *Will Penny*, chronicles the life of a veteran cowboy. But the emphasis here is not on the hardships but rather on the fullness and dignity of cowboy life. The credits of *Monte Walsh* are shown imposed over drawings of cowboys by Charles Russell. These drawings set the tone for the entire movie. Throughout the film, cinematographer David Walsh carefully composes shots of the land, horses, cattle and groups of cowboys to look like Russell's paintings and drawings. Thus, the day-to-day life of Monte (Lee Marvin) and the other cowboys, which takes up most of the picture, is made to look permanent and beautiful.

Most of the film is quiet and gentle. The close relationship between Monte and his saddle partner, Chet Rollins (Jack Palance), is shown by having Monte continually take Chet's pipe tobacco so Monte can roll a cigarette. The humor of bunkhouse life is depicted by having the cowboys make the cook take a bath. The relationship between man and land is shown by the camera's simply sweeping back to show a man tending fence on the vast empty plain. The two most interesting high points of the film are not slam-bang shoot-outs, but actions entirely likely in a cowboy's life. In one, Monte proves to himself that he is still a man of dignity by riding a horse that had previously bucked off everyone else on the ranch. In the other, Monte tells his girl, Martine (Jean Moreau), whom he deeply loves, that he won't marry her because he can only be a cowboy, and being a cowboy, he cannot support her.

The fourth type of contemporary Western, the personal-Western, resembles the new-Western in its tendency to wander from the Western formula into other themes and sets of motivations. Foremost in a personal-Western is the individual vision of the director. But unlike films such as *Will Penny*, personal-Westerns continue to be constructed around the epic moment and violent-but-honorable hero of the traditional-Western.

There have of course always been personal-Westerns. The *auteur* critics have discovered deeply personal philosophies and attitudes in the Westerns of Fritz Lang, Samuel Fuller, Budd Boetticher, and many others. The directors of older personal-Westerns, however, kept the formula at the forefront and inserted their own ideas as embellishments. John Ford, for example, attempted to build a historical mythos of the West centered on a compassionate, often sentimental affirmation of the structure of the family. Howard Hawks, on the other hand, has always been obsessed with tests of strength and honor, and the communion between brave, virile men. Yet, in 1949, these two very different directors each made a Western, Ford's *She Wore a Yellow Ribbon* and Hawks' *Red River*, in which the same woman, Joanne Dru, unites the same older hero, John Wayne, with younger men in order to preserve peace on the newly settled frontier. No such similarities of construction would be possible in the contemporary personal-Western. Unlike older directors such as Ford and Hawks, new directors such as Sam Peckinpah and Robert Altman build their movies primarily around their singular interpretations of the human experience and use the Western formula only as a point of reference. Consequently, their films tend to be confusing, and are often analyzed as anti-Westerns. The accusation that Sam Peckinpah's vast panorama of blood, *The Wild Bunch* (1969), is an anti-Western seems at first glance to be obviously justified. Both the social world and the protagonists of *The Wild Bunch* appear to be almost demonically sadistic and corrupt. The film opens with children torturing scorpions by covering them with ants. Later, they just as pleasurably help torture Angel, the youngest member of the Wild Bunch. Still later it is a child who finally kills the oldest member of the gang, Pike Bishop (William Holden). These children have obviously learned their lesson in cruelty from the adults of the film. Motherhood is symbolized by a woman giving suck to her child while wearing a gunbelt across her chest. And the posse, in the conventional-Western usually seen as protector of the town, in *The Wild Bunch* shoots down nearly a dozen innocent people in one town and, at the end of the picture, like a flock of gluttonous vultures robs the bodies of the slain inhabitants of a second town. The members of the Wild Bunch seem to be little better. Killing becomes an inevitable part of their two robberies in the film and several times they are on the verge of murdering one another.

Underneath their natural brutality, however, the members of the Bunch have their own strong code of honor based on personal loyalty. Bishop summarizes this in the best known lines of the film when he says to the gang, "We're gonna stick together, all of us . . . When you side with a man you stay with him. If you can't do that you're worse than some animal." Pike's closest friend, Dutch (Ernest Borgnine), says nearly the same thing later when he insists, "It don't matter [if you give your word]. It's who you give your word to." The moral crisis of the film occurs when Angel is captured by the Mexican bandit Mapache. At first the Bunch decide to leave Angel. But their consciences draw them first into Mapache's village and finally, against great numbers of Mapache's men, to demand Angel's release. When Angel is killed by Mapache, the Bunch retaliate and finally, before they themselves are shot down, they seize a machine gun and slaughter dozens of Mapache's people. The Bunch all die smiling, however. Their violent last act is only what is natural in the bestial world of Sam Peckinpah.

Their smiles are for their free consciences. They have been true to their code of loyalty.

Peckinpah thus keeps *The Wild Bunch* within the conventions of the Western formula. Normally, the code of criminals leads to the destruction of society. But Peckinpah's personal interpretation of society reverses this relationship. In the nihilistic world of *The Wild Bunch* the only evidence of civilization is the code of loyalty the members of the Bunch have for each other. In their final suicidal shoot-out, they obtain heroic stature by using their guns in defense of that code.

In *McCabe and Mrs. Miller* (1971) director Robert Altman, like Sam Peckinpah, creates a very personal world in which to play out a traditional Western tale. John McCabe (Warren Beatty) is unlike the usual rugged he-man hero of an ordinary Western. He more closely resembles a modern oily-tongued used-car salesman. McCabe's initial method of making money is to tell good dirty jokes in order to lure men into a poker game. He becomes a town leader by opening up the town's first whorehouse and promising women who "can do more tricks than a goddamn monkey on a hundred yards of grape vine."

McCabe may be a vulgar and rather small-time operator but Altman creates an environment and set of circumstances which elevate McCabe to the stature of hero. At the beginning of the film, as McCabe rides into the town of Presbyterian Church he passes the church itself, and we see that it is obviously being neglected. It stands empty and only half built. As Leonard Cohen, on the soundtrack, sings about a "Joseph looking for a manger," McCabe dismounts and goes into Tim Sheehan's bar. Here lies the real Church. Sheehan lights a candle in front of a statue of the Virgin. McCabe sets out an altar by spreading a red blanket on a barroom table. As Cohen sings about "the sacred game of poker," McCabe smoothly tells his jokes and stories. The high point of what is a ritual of the poker table comes when McCabe pulls a silver whiskey flask from his pocket and passes it to the players around the table. McCabe is, therefore, a Christ-priest figure, and, indeed he does help save the town. When McCabe opens his own bar and sporting-house he brings a sudden atmosphere of properly domesticated prosperity to Presbyterian Church. Filthy miners begin to take frequent baths in order to visit McCabe's "ladies." Solid frame buildings go up. And the first women arrive who intend to marry and settle. As a redeemer of the community McCabe plays a vital function in bringing a rough section of frontier Washington State under civilized control. In doing so he is fulfilling the normal role of the Western hero.

McCabe obtains even more solid hero status at the end of the film when he defends the town against hired killers in a traditional Western shoot-out. The reasons for McCabe's willingness to fight the hired guns of the Bearpaw Mining Company seem personal; the mining company intends to kill him and take his property. Everyone else in town has settled with them already. But McCabe's reasons for staying are not selfish. He refuses the chance to sneak out of town and escape the killers athough, as he has earlier told Sheehan, in another town when problems arose he did pick up and leave. McCabe stays because he is convinced it is his duty to stay. A lawyer has talked him into believing that the Bearpaw Mining Company is a ruthless exploiter of the "small businessman . . . the soul of this great nation," and that he, John McCabe, must help stop them. Furthermore, McCabe is hopelessly in love with his partner in the sportinghouse, Constance Miller (Julie Christie). In a touching soliloquy the night before the gunfight he admits to himself that he deeply loves her and despairs that she has humiliated him by refusing to return his love. Like a knight sharpening his sword to chivalrously defend the property of the lady he has sworn fealty to, McCabe speaks his soliloquy while loading his six-shooter. In the gunfight itself McCabe proves fully the equal of traditional heroes. Like Shane, he is fatally wounded, but is nevertheless able to first kill all three of his adversaries.

Even though the Western formula is still adhered to and respected in the new personal-Westerns, it is not necessarily for the purpose of affirming the experience of the great American settlement of the vast land, as is the intent of the traditional Western. The formula in the personal-Western is merely one device among many for creating the viewpoint of the director. For Sam Peckinpah, the heroism of the Wild Bunch is in part ironic. In a violent world their willingness to defend a code of loyalty leads to a final act of carnage much more horrifying than any perpetrated by all those characters in the film who are without a code of morality. For Robert Altman, McCabe's face-off with three professional killers is tragicomedy. McCabe is a Western hero because he has fallen for the outrageous patriotic clichés of a lawyer and the attentions of a Cockney opium-smoking whore.

II

If the formula of current Western movies resembles the pellets from a discharged shotgun, the gunpowder blasting out those pellets is the terrifying oncoming of modernization. Older Westerns attempted to create around their stories an aura of regeneration and timelessness. Invariably the heroes of "B" Westerns rode out of town at film's end leaving the audience with the understanding that the next time trouble occurred, the hero would return to perform his skilled and violent services. Such an understanding ceased to exist in the sixties. In John Ford's *The Man Who Shot Liberty Valance* (1962), for example, an Eastern dude lawyer, Ransom Stoddard, takes over as community

leader from old-fashioned Western man of action Tom Doniphon
(John Wayne). And in David Miller's *Lonely Are the Brave* (1962),
Kirk Douglas' fight to remain a free roamer abruptly ends when his
horse is run down by a truck carrying a load of toilets. Increasingly,
Western movie makers are becoming less interested in the traditional
epic moment when the pioneer stood eyeball to eyeball with nature,
and more and more obsessed with the multivaried tensions contained
within a new moment in history when progress overcame the fundamental aspirations of the old pioneer and transformed him into someone suddenly irrelevant and out of place. So predominant has this new
theme of time as a traitor to Western legends become that it is itself
becoming almost a new formula within which all forms of the scattered versions of the old formula are contained.

The passage of time has done the most obvious damage to the traditional Western. It shows its presence in the gray hairs and wrinkling
faces of the old-time Western stars who are usually still the featured
performers. What makes Valdez an interesting character in *Valdez Is
Coming* is Burt Lancaster's old age. Lancaster plays Valdez as a man
near fifty whose favorite companion is not a lusty young adventurer
but a philosophical old man of the village. When Valdez puts on his
old cavalry scout clothes and begins his revenge we understand it not
as an endlessly repeated act, but as a glorious last fling.

With no regeneration, traditional Westerns cannot long continue.
Mark Rydell's *The Cowboys* (1971) attempts to recreate heroes by the
passing on of a sacred legacy. Rancher Wil Andersen (John Wayne)
hires eleven young boys to help him on a cattle drive. During the drive
Andersen teaches the boys about individualism, bravery and hard work.
When Andersen is killed by rustlers the boys assume his heroic role.
They kill the rustlers and deliver the cattle to market. At the film's
conclusion, the boys return to Andersen's grave to find it has disappeared. As a type of frontier Christ, John Wayne has delivered the
gospel and ascended into heaven leaving eleven young apostles to
spread the message. Unfortunately, the regeneration of the cowboy in
such young lads remains doubtful. It might be remembered that another gutsy independent youngster, Mattie Ross of Charles Portis'
novel *True Grit*, grew up to be a miserly old maid banker whose
greatest pleasure was foreclosing mortgages. *The Cowboys* is meant as
a message of hope for lovers of old Westerns. Yet perhaps the most
memorable moment in the film occurs when John Wayne tells his
screen wife that he is sixty years old. It is a shocking admission. As we
hear Wayne say it we become fully aware that he *is* getting old. If this
greatest of all Western heroes can age and die, so, obviously, can all
others. Time has therefore finally caught up to and is destroying the
Western myth of the eternally recurring moment of heroic action.

The new-Western, since it is the freest of the four types of the West-

ern formula, should also be free from the tension of age and mo-
dernity. But, so far, the major new-Westerns are also fascinated with
the theme of the treachery of time. Will Penny dreams all his life of
a good wife and warm hearth. However, at the conclusion of *Will
Penny,* when the woman he has rescued begs him to stay with her, Will
says, "I'm damn near fifty years old. What could we do? . . . It's too
late . . . too late for me." In *Monte Walsh,* although Monte is not
much younger than Will Penny, it is the times, not age, that destroy
him. Jack Schaeffer's long novel upon which the movie is based chronicled Monte's life from the time of his childhood to his death. The film
ignores most of Monte's life, and concentrates on the years 1888–89,
the years when blizzards and droughts forced most independent ranchers out of business and spelled an end to the free open-range life of
thousands of cowhands. Monte is one of the victims of the elements.
At the end of the movie, he is alone and out of work. Stumbling across
a wolf, he pulls out a rifle and takes aim, but decides not to shoot.
Monte and the wolf are brothers, two lonely, obsolete, wild things on
ranch land which will be made more productive by Eastern industrial
business methods and efficiency.

Anti-Westerns do not treat a specific moment when one era ended
and another began. They prefer to make broader boundaries between
conflicting zones of time. In an anti-Western, the central tension is invariably between a cynical contemporary knowledge of the horrors of
the Westward movement and past idealism about the glories of the
great Western migration. *Hombre* becomes more biting when we realize that without their moral degeneracy the characters might be very
much like the archetypal Westerners in John Ford's *Stagecoach.* Because they are primarily interested in exposing the disparity between
the historically real West and the historically fantasized West, it is not
surprising that many anti-Westerns, among them *Soldier Blue* (1970),
Doc (1971), *Little Big Man* (1971) and *Dirty Little Billy* (1972) are
based on actual historical incidents.

Sam Peckinpah and Robert Altman make changing eras a central
theme in their personal-Westerns *The Wild Bunch* and *McCabe and
Mrs. Miller* by moving the time for the traditional Western (1866–89)
one generation ahead to 1913 and 1902 respectively.

"We gotta start thinking beyond our guns. Them days is closin' fast,"
Pike Bishop tells his gang in *The Wild Bunch.* Such a change, however, would be impossible for them. Their old-fashioned code puts
them hopelessly out of touch with an honorless modern world on the
brink of World War One. When Angel is captured by Mapache, Angel
is tortured by being dragged by an automobile, a symbol of an increasingly complex mode of living that tortures all the members of the
Bunch. When the Bunch grab the machine gun at the film's bloody
climax and use it to slaughter scores of Mapache's henchmen, the ma-

chine gun becomes a symbol of triumphant defiance not unlike Ahab's harpoon in *Moby Dick*. It is a gun and their use of it in relation to Bishop's earlier statement shows a refusal to change, a violent insistence upon remaining true to what they have always thought best in themselves. The machine gun is also a modern weapon. By turning it on their oppressors they are able to use for revenge a symbol of modern life which, like the automobile, is a part of the incomprehensible new world that ultimately destroys them. Like Ahab dying on the back of the white whale he hated because he could not fully understand it, the Wild Bunch die fighting and destroying Mapache's village because they can never be a part of it.

Robert Altman's reaction to the passing away of the relevancy of the epic moment is not a violent curse of rage like *The Wild Bunch*. Altman bows to the inevitable; his John McCabe dies quietly and all alone in the softly falling snow. While McCabe is fighting the hired guns of the mining company, the townspeople have all rallied together on the other side of town to save the burning frame of the Presbyterian Church. The townspeople's sudden interest in the church they ignored throughout the rest of the film shows that the town itself has changed. It is suddenly more sophisticated and domestic. Worship services will no longer be bawdy poker games at Sheehan's bar but instead will take place inside the church the townspeople vow to rebuild. Big industry will take over the town. Prosperity will come. A school will be built. Nobody sees McCabe fight the hired guns of the mining company. Nobody cares. In McCabe's moment of greatest heroism, history has turned a screw, and his heroism has become meaningless.

III

In the 1960's and 70's, by spreading into several new directions, Westerns have demonstrated that another aspect of their extraordinary longevity is their capacity to creatively embrace a wide spectrum of ideas and aesthetic constructions. Personal-Westerns such as *McCabe and Mrs. Miller* and *The Wild Bunch* have been acclaimed as classics at the same time five millon dollars were being spent to create an epic panorama for John Wayne in a traditional Western, *The Cowboys*. Important young writers and directors are returning to the Western to find within it a rich source for their varying visions. John Milius has written two successful Western scripts attempting to re-establish Western heroism, *The Life and Times of Judge Roy Bean* (1972) and *Jeremiah Johnson* (1972). Peter Fonda chose for his initiation into movie directing a new-Western, *The Hired Hand* (1971). And Clint Eastwood, the most important Western star in a generation, directed a striking personal-Western, *High Plains Drifter* (1973).

Despite the pleasant cowboy melodies being sung by Western director night-herders, storm clouds keep gathering. The herd is restless and threatening to stampede. While on one hand the spreading out of the Western formula undoubtedly has added to the rich possibilities open to the creators of Westerns, on the other hand the fragmenting of the genre itself illustrates some disturbing truths about the mood of the people in contemporary America. The Western, as does any popular story formula, embodies the most essential wishes, hopes and beliefs of the people that have produced it. Consequently, as perhaps the most purely native American story form, the Western may be looked upon as a metaphor of the American culture out of which it grew. The blasting out of the Western story into new directions and into new forms in contemporary Western movies therefore reflects a similar splitting in the American consciousness.

The scattered Western formula symbolizes the most prevalent tensions and contradictions in American society. Anti-Westerns reflect the same intellectual disillusionment with the process of the great American settlement that has become a standard attitude among revisionist historians in academia. Against this liberal cynicism is the diehard belief in old-fashioned individualism found in the traditional-Westerns. The restless return to the agrarian myth by young people who grow organic food and move into communes is reflected in the respectful study of cowboy life in the new-Westerns. And all of these themes —old versus new; agrarianism versus a growing technocracy; cynicism versus idealism—provide the thematic framework for the makers of personal-Westerns.

The importance of understanding what has happened to the Western formula lies in what such a study reveals about the depth and degree of the ideological fragmentation of American society that began in the 1960's. For sixty years, through three wars and a depression, the movies' unified myth of the West was able to satisfactorily articulate the purpose and the worthiness of the American experience. Now those myths have run up against the social and political nightmares of the 60's and 70's and that heretofore solid vision has exploded into pieces. If the Western is truly an indicator of American beliefs, the American's vision of himself as an indomitable Adam in the new Eden, virtuous in doing God's work of taming the wild land, is gone forever. The new theme of the past in conflict with the present in nearly all contemporary Westerns reveals the desperate emptiness left by the loss of this vision. Without a vision where is purpose? Where is meaning? If the myth of the old Western was a false one, the scattered search of contemporary Westerns for the meaning of the moment when the old Western ideals died reveals an intense present-day American quest for the discovery of another epic moment in American history from which may come a new, more meaningful American mythos.

Reflections on the New Western Films
by JOHN G. CAWELTI

Since the middle 1960s, it has been difficult to speak of a single western formula. As Jack Nachbar puts it in his essay on the recent western, the classic formula of regeneration has been scattered in several different directions. The only single trend that seems to mark the many different sorts of western is an emphasis on the graphic portrayal of violence, as opposed to the more bloodless and acrobatic deaths of the preceding period, together with a more explicit indication of the role of sex in the stories. This is hardly surprising since it reflects a general trend in American culture and is not by any means unique to the western.

Indeed, as Robert Warshow pointed out in his superb essay on the classic western, one important aspect of the western is that it is one of the few art forms in our culture that has consistently attempted a serious treatment of violence. This current interest on the part of film makers in a more intense portrayal of violence, and the audience response to that representation, may be in part a catering to jaded and corrupted taste; but, more importantly, I feel, this emphasis grows out of a need to arrive at some understanding of the new and terrifying mood of destructiveness and hate, not only in America, but in the world as a whole.

The classic westerns of the 1940s and 1950s depended on and reaffirmed for us the traditional American view that violence was the fault of evil and corrupt men; good men might be forced to use it in purging society of corruption, but this would lead to a regenerated social order. With the fading of this hope and the growing sense of danger from personal and collective violence in our society, Americans have had to come to some kind of emotional terms with an unregenerate world. By looking at some of the diverse trends in the westerns of today we can define some of the new attitudes toward violence which are emerging.

From The University of Chicago Magazine (*January–February 1973*), *pp. 26–30, 32. The full version of this essay appears on pp. 25–32. Reprinted by permission of the author.*

The most widely imitated of the new western formulas was created by the Italian director Sergio Leone in a tremendously popular series of films mainly starring Clint Eastwood—*A Fistful of Dollars* (1966); *For a Few Dollars More* (1966); *The Good, the Bad and the Ugly* (1967); *Once Upon a Time in the West* (1969).

The films of Leone and his imitators are full of violent action like the traditional B westerns, but in other respects they represent a major departure in theme, story and style from the tradition. Their plots resemble Jacobean or Spanish Renaissance tragedy more than they do the traditional western, and so does their vision of a dark, corrupt, and treacherous world. Their ostensible heroes are marked not by moral purpose and righteous courage, but by superior stratagems, unscrupulousness, and skill in violence. Their style, embodied in leading actors like Clint Eastwood and Lee Van Cleef, is one of supreme detachment and coolness.

Eastwood as "the man with no name"—an anonymity which underlines his lack of human feeling and motive—performs his most violent deeds without a quiver of his characteristic cigarillo or a ripple of his serape. His role in a number of the films is that of bounty hunter, the man who kills with no personal interest but the monetary reward—a despicable occupation in the moral universe of the traditional western.

If the hero has any motive beyond money, it is usually to perform some terrible revenge for a long-past deed, a revenge which commonly seems more like a dehumanizing obsession than a justifiable moral purpose.

In many cases, the object of the hero's revenge is as interesting and sympathetic a character as he is, if not more so. In *Once Upon a Time in the West*, for example, the "villain" is played by Henry Fonda, the hero of many traditional westerns, and the "hero" by Charles Bronson, who had earlier made a specialty of villains. With such heroes, one asks, who needs villains? Yet the Leone films do successfully arouse our interest in the hero's actions, despite his morally ambiguous character, by showing us a world that seems to deserve whatever violence can be wreaked upon it.

Because the world is violent, treacherous, and corrupt, the moral man is the one who can use violence, treachery, and corruption most effectively. The chief thing that differentiates hero from villain is the hero's coolness and lack of violent emotion; the villain is typically given to rages of greed, lust, or hatred which prevent him from effectively using the tools of power.

Public enthusiasm for the Leone films has commonly been interpreted as a simple response of salacious sadism, the cruder masses of the public taking lip-licking delight in the vivid portrayal of wounding and death.

No doubt there are such appeals in the Leone films. Anyone who has attended one of these films in company with a large and varied audience can testify to what seems at first a shocking ghoulishness of response—applause when an innocent person is destroyed on screen, laughter at the most horrible kind of maiming and killing. One could easily become convinced that such films are creating a bloodthirsty public who will eventually turn from fantasy to reality to satisfy their cravings. Yet, the fact is that few Clint Eastwood fans, if any, become mass murderers.

Despite almost two decades of research of various kinds, it has not been possible to demonstrate convincingly that violence in films incites people to violent actions in real life. This should lead us to wonder if the orientation toward violence in the Leone films is as simple as it seems on the surface.

On closer examination I should say that these films perhaps appeal as much to a sense of passivity as to violence. Their grotesque humor may well be more an invitation to laugh at our own sense of helplessness and victimization than an incitement to strike out against it. Their moral ambiguity, their rejection of clear distinctions between hero and villain, and their effects of grotesque horror might just as well be interpreted as an attempt to transform our sense of moral paralysis and impotence in the face of worldwide violence into mockery and bitter comedy.

If this is the case, we have here one new kind of thematic portrayal of violence, together with an implicit psychological strategy toward it. Violence is innate in human life, and the only defense against it is detached mockery. By avoiding emotional and moral involvement, we develop a capacity to gain pleasure from horror and outrage through identification with victmizer as well as victim.

This attitude is close to the one implicit in the contemporary horror film—the current crop of Draculas, Blaculas, Frankensteins, and Wolfmen—where we are invited to identify with the monster as well as with those he victimizes, in contrast to the traditional horror story, where the monster represented an outside evil that had to be purged to save the world. Like the Italian western, which it resembles in its grotesque tone and its cultivation of horrific incident, the new-style horror film has been one of the great popular successes of the past two decades.

The distinctive quality of the Leone western emerges in another way when we compare it with another type of contemporary western, a formula that might be called the return of the rugged individual. These films, dominantly starring John Wayne, have been strongly influenced by certain aspects of the Italian western, but are generally attempts to restate the traditional western themes in a slightly new fashion.

Typically, this second type of contemporary western deals with an aging hero, whose great days seem over but who embarks upon one more heroic quest or battle. Unlike the Italian western, this American type portrays the hero's quest as the pursuit of a clearly moral purpose. In *True Grit*, the hero is a marshal who has been employed by a young lady to bring in the murderer of her father. In *Big Jake*, his grandson has been kidnapped by a band of outlaws and he is out to recover the child; in *Chisum*, corrupt and lawless men threaten to destroy the peaceful cattle empire which John Chisum has built up through hard work and honest dealing. Similar plot devices ensure that the deeds of the protagonists of *Rio Lobo* and *The Cowboys* are covered with the mantle of morality.

But in many ways this air of morality seems more like a ritual than a reality, a cloak for naked aggression, rather than the reluctant violence of the heroes of *My Darling Clementine*, *High Noon*, and *Shane*. The leading figure in these rugged individualist westerns is very different in his qualities from the lyrical or stoic heroes of the 1940s and 1950s. In fact, he resembles the official villains of the earlier westerns as much as he does the heroes.

John Chisum is an overbearing cattle baron, like Ryker, the villain of *Shane*. Big Jake has the same ruthlessness and love-hate relationship with his sons as the maniacal Dock Tobin of Anthony Mann's *Man of the West*, while the *Wild Bunch* of Sam Peckinpah's film bears more resemblance to the vicious Clanton gang than to the gentle Wyatt Earp of *My Darling Clementine*.

Yet, in these newer romances of rugged individualism in the West, the ruthless aggressiveness, concern with power, and penchant for violence, which were seen as dangerous and even evil in the classic westerns, are portrayed as positive values or moral necessities. To make the contrast more precise, we might compare Howard Hawks' *Red River* (1948) and the recent *Chisum*. These two films have basic plot similarities and in both the central figure is played by John Wayne. However, in *Red River* Wayne's overbearing individualism, his tyrannical authority, and his ruthless appeals to violence nearly bring about destruction of the cattle drive. It is only the rejection of violence and the concern for the welfare of others embodied in the secondary hero figure of Wayne's adopted son, played by Montgomery Clift, that finally resolves the difficulties.

But in *Chisum* these very aggressive qualities make the hero successful, while the more pacific and less domineering temperaments of younger men are shown to be inadequate to the overcoming of evil.

In none of these films is there much question of group regeneration associated with the hero's purging action. On the contrary, society is usually represented as weak and corrupt; its agencies, like posses and armed forces, are given to impulsive and inefficient violence which is more likely to bring on further innocent suffering than to establish true justice. Because society is violent and corrupt, the only solution lies in the private action of a good leader who is able to overcome the outlaw's evil aggression and society's own endemic violence and corruption by superior ruthlessness and power of his own.

In this emphasis on the failure of society to protect the innocent and on the need for the private leader and avenger, these new westerns clearly resemble the new gangster film and novel exemplified in *The Godfather*. I should say that the orientation toward violence and society is almost identical in these works. Because society has failed to extend its protection and order to an adequate extent, the little man is constantly threatened by violence against which he cannot protect himself.

The fantasied solution is to fall back on the Godfather—or, in the case of the western, on the grandfather, Big Jake—and to create under his absolute authority a close-knit small group, like a family, which in return for absolute loyalty will protect its members.

The two new western types I have discussed—the Italian western and the western Godfather—share a disillusioned and pessimistic view of society and an obsession with the place of violence in it. As the western has always done, these new formulas project the tensions and concerns of the present into the legendary past in order to seek in the imagination some kind of resolution or acceptance of conflicts of value and feeling which cannot be solved in the present.

Who Are Those Guys?
The Movie Western
During the TV Era
by RALPH BRAUER

If a frog had wings he wouldn't bump his ass so much—

MC CABE IN ALTMAN'S
McCabe and Mrs. Miller

These are cats who ran out of territory and know it. But they don't bend, refuse to be diminished by it. They play their string out to the end—

SAM PECKINPAH ON HIS FILM
Pat Garrett and Billy the Kid

Several years ago Bob Dylan put out an album called *John Wesley Harding,* one of the seminal documents for those who want to understand the past decade and what it has meant to many of us who have been styled the youth generation. The title song of *John Wesley Harding* was a song about a western gunfighter who was a friend to the poor and who was never known to hurt an honest man.

In 1973 Dylan found himself playing a knife-throwing character named Alias, a member of a gang led by Billy the Kid (played by another troubador, Kris Kristofferson) in Sam Peckinpah's *Pat Garrett and Billy the Kid.* Peckinpah's Billy is a lot like Dylan's John Wesley Harding, except that Billy is doomed to die, doomed by the very forces which Dylan lashed out against in his many albums and songs—the businessmen, the politicians, the "silent-majority" townspeople types, and the holier-than-thou, with-God-on-our-siders.

From The Journal of Popular Film, *vol. 2, no. 3 (Fall 1973), 389–404. Reprinted by permission of the publisher.*

Peckinpah's movie is not the equal of his earlier masterpieces *The Wild Bunch* and the neglected *The Ballad of Cable Hogue,* but it was a stroke of sheer genius to cast Dylan and Kristofferson in the roles of Billy and Alias for in doing this he endowed the film with a host of additional meanings that would not have been possible if he had used "normal" actors. To those of us who have listened to the work of both song writers as a way of perhaps finding sanity in a world gone mad with Vietnam, assassinations, and the ugly head of fascism that looms behind Watergate, we cannot help but see the Dylan-Kristofferson roles in this larger context. Peckinpah has made it more difficult for us not to do this with his use of Dylan singing the title song for the movie, a song a great deal like *John Wesley Harding's* title song. Kristofferson-Billy-John Welsey Harding dies, but Dylan-Alias lives, the wise fool whose wisdom may yet save us all.

Peckinpah's casting may well have been his most brilliant stroke for not only has he used Dylan and Kristofferson, but a host of old-time Western actors, each of whose previous roles seem to endow the present film with additional power. There is Jason Robards, Cable Hogue, risen to the position of governor of New Mexico; Slim Pickens as an old sheriff; and Jack Elam, an old badman who hires on as Garrett's deputy. Then there's James Coburn, the superstud of those horrible *Flint* films—the establishment's hired gun, playing a Pat Garrett who sells out to the establishment because he can see the handwriting on the wall.

And what is the handwriting he sees? Well, actually it's something that not only Peckinpah but several other Western directors of the sixties have seen: a vision of closing options, of men run out of territory, of mass society, corporate America, killing the individual.

The idea of closing options is not a new one with Peckinpah or even with the sixties, for in many ways it grew out of the Westerns of the forties and fifties—the Westerns which critics have referred to as "serious Westerns."

In most discussions of the Western it is standard to refer to the "serious" Western of the forties and fifties as representing a "new wave" in the Western, as being more critical or complex. Some critics like to refer to this as the period when the Western "grew up." Some of this is intellectual bunk; some of it is also a sort of snobbish reaction by critics who for some reason or another could not get into Mix, Hart, Buck Jones, Tim McCoy, etc. The new "serious" Western became *the* Western for another generation and Tim McCoy and Ken Maynard were relegated to showings on Saturday afternoon TV kiddie shows.

When these critics speak of the "serious" Westerns of the forties and fifties, they usually begin with *Stagecoach* and go on to include such "classics" as *High Noon, Shane,* and *The Gunfighter.*

Westerns are our fables of identity, our national "epics" in which we express the complexities and ambiguities of our own existence. According to many critics what the so-called "serious" Westerns of the forties and fifties did was to examine critically some of the elements of earlier Westerns, such as the gunfighter, as well as broaden the subject matter into what Fenin and Everson call "sex, neurosis and a racial conscience." [1]

Of the serious Westerns of the fifties, *Shane, The Gunfighter,* and *The Left-Handed Gun* are usually cited as among the best. Jon Tuska of *Views and Reviews* said on his NET documentary "They Went Thata Way" that he thought *Shane* (1953) was *the* best Western. Perhaps it is indicative of our respective generations that Tuska picked for his choice what I consider a nostalgic vision, while I would pick the more violent *The Wild Bunch.* Why do I say *Shane* is a nostalgic vision when I just finished saying the critics had called it a "serious" Western? I think all of these qualities are wrapped up in the famous ending. After the stranger with only one name has cleaned up the baddies, he rides off into the mist with the small boy's shouting of his name echoing in the mountains beyond. It has often been pointed out that this scene has a visionary quality about it, as if the whole movie and our whole idea of the West were only a small boy's dream. Hence *Shane* is a "serious" Western. Certainly the ending is a beautiful touch, but I question whether it is as critical as many seem to think. Perhaps it is the quality of Stevens' color or his location that lead me to call it nostalgic. Stevens' color reminds me of the color which we have come to associate with the romanticism of *Elvira Madigan* and similar pictures. It is a nostalgic color, a sort of picture postcard color. I often wonder how much the picture would have been changed if it had been shot in black and white. In line with Stevens' color it is interesting to note how Altman uses color in *McCabe and Mrs. Miller.* In *McCabe* the color becomes more "clear" as the picture progresses. It is almost like *Shane* turned upside down. The *Shane* location, Jackson Hole, also seems to add to the nostalgic feeling. Finally there is the *Shane* plot. The *Shane* plot is stock B-Western stuff, down to the gunfighter dressed in black. Only Jack Palance's portrayal saves his role from seeming absurd. That to me is the essence of *Shane.* It seems always threatening to dissolve into banality, but always recovers. What redeems it finally is the ending, the little boy shouting. *Shane* is the ideal Western for a generation of critics who relegated Ken Maynard to a Saturday TV matinee and then secretly watched him themselves— wishing they could be kids again at the Saturday Picture Show with popcorn and a double feature all for only a dime.

The Gunfighter (1950) does not seem to differ too greatly from *Shane.* Gregory Peck plays an old gunfighter returned to visit his wife and see

[1] George Fenin and William K. Everson, *The Western.* New York: Orion Press, 1962, p. 265–66.

pain of America brought alive on the screen." 3 What Kitses says of Peckinpah might just as well be said of Hellman and Altman.

This quality of present igniting the past can be seen in Peckinpah and Altman's portrayals of Wringle-like conniving businessmen. In Peckinpah's *The Ballad of Cable Hogue*, Hogue stumbles on a water-hole that lies along the long trail winding through the desert between two towns and proceeds to get rich selling water to thirsty travelers. In Altman's *McCabe and Mrs. Miller*, McCabe ends up controlling a whole town, building whorehouses, gambling halls, hotels, baths, etc. Unlike Ford's Wringle, Peckinpah and Altman's businessman types are he "heroes" of the film, and unlike Ford, Peckinpah and Altman eem to intimate that the businessman grew out of American individuism and in turn spawned the corporations of the anti-individualistic entieth century. The freewheeling outlawry of the Wild Bunch ves way to the militaristic, uniformed outlawry of Mapache; the busissman Hogue dies under the wheels of an automobile produced by a poration and world he cannot understand; and McCabe dies alone the snow after fighting off the paid goons of the corporation that tually will control "his" town. Mapache is actually only a more nized, less individualistic version of the Bunch; the automobile h now makes Hogue and his waterhole obsolete grew from a simimpulse to make money from travelers on the trail—where Hogue's hole stood there is now probably a Holiday Inn, a few gas stamaybe a public campground for those pickup campers that clog ighways—and McCabe's town gives way to the corporation town: mestead and Park Forest and Levittown, to shopping centers, n movies, and a society that is rapidly making one of McCabe's makers, whoring, obsolete and the other, gambling, a state conor a Mafia monopoly.

these directors do in different degrees and for different reasons sh the idea of open options to its limits so that we are left with bing sense that it is an idea which has lost its validity. In the Peckinpah, Hellman, and Altman the options are closing and o believe them to be open or who fight to keep them open are o suffer the most. In a sense their work is a Western Turner where Turner spoke of the closing of the historical frontier ctors speak eloquently of the closing of a mythical, thematic

hree it is Altman who is the most bleak, Hellman the most with Peckinpah somewhere in between. For this reason is the most interesting, as well as the most profound of these im Kitses has called Peckinpah "John Ford's bastard son," 4

163-69.
9.

---

the son he has not seen for so long in a town whose sheriff is an old friend. The picture attempts to deromanticize the gunfighter figure, who does not like the life he must lead, but who leads it because it is his life. In the end he is killed, in an unfair fight, by a punk kid who wants the reputation of having shot Jimmy Ringo. As he lies dying in the street Ringo turns to the boy and tells him that, rather than have him arrested, he will let the boy live with his reputation, that now the boy must live the sordid life of a gunfighter. Again the critics have spoken of this as a "serious" critical Western. Again I would say that it is, in a sense, but that it still retains elements of nostalgia and sentimentality. *The Gunfighter* reminds me a lot of those anti-movies they showed us in high school. In some ways it is even like some of those so-called anti-drug commercials being shown now on TV. The idea of all these movies and commercials is that we are not supposed to play chicken with hot rods, go "all the way," drink, smoke, use dope. The idea is that after seeing *The Gunfighter,* we are supposed to be rid of our wishes to be gunfighters, because after all it is a sordid life, you cannot have a family, and you end up dead before your time. It sounds good but it does not work any more than it does in those old high-school films. If everyone who saw *The Gunfighter* had to pick out a role in the movie to play, he would pick the Gregory Peck role. There is something about the all-or-nothing daredevil that appeals to Americans. *The Gunfighter* merely celebrates this myth, it does not come to any critical understanding of it.

There were, of course, other Westerns during the forties and fifties, yet most of them fall into the same pattern. *The Outlaw* (1943), often described as the first Western with sex and sadism, contains a sentimental ending not unlike that of *Shane. Run For Cover* (1955) uses the old stock plot of men accused of a crime they didn't commit, but contains none of the paranoia of Monte Hellman's 1965 variation of the theme, *Ride in the Whirlwind. Run For Cover* ends with the hero and heroine walking through the crowd of townspeople. In Anthony Mann's *Man of the West* (1958) the reformed outlaw is forced to reject his schoolteacher wife and his new identity as a "respectable" member of society, but in the end rides off into the sunset with the girl—like John Wayne in *Stagecoach* (1939).

So where does this leave us with the so-called "serious" Western? I think if one were to sum up these Westerns with one word, it would be the word used to describe *Shane*—nostalgic. The protagonists of these Westerns are all portrayed sympathetically, but it is a sympathy tinged with nostalgia. Shane may be only a figment of a little boy's imagination and the gunfighter may not lead the life he does in "B" Westerns but still they are figures we know and feel drawn toward. Perhaps John Ford, probably our greatest director—not only of Westerns—caught the attitude of the fifties Westerns best in his late Westerns *The Man Who Shot Liberty Valance* (1962) and *Two Rode Together* (1961). For Ford the Western and the Western myth seemed to have lost their meaning or had been expropriated by politicians and perverted by businessmen. As James Stewart put it in *Two Rode Together*, "The trouble is there [are] too many Wringles in this world today." (Wringle is a conniving businessman.) What we have in the fifties Western is not a criticism of Shane or the gunfighter or the mixed-up teen-ager, but a feeling that these figures are now threatened, that they are ultimately very vulnerable, that that was once a pure vision of the West is being undermined by Wringles and other assorted figures and forces. It is the sixties Westerns which go beyond this nostalgia to a deep sense of closing options, and, in some cases, to show how Wringle and the Western are more than mere antitheses.

In these sixties Westerns, the Western seems to be searching for a new definition of ourselves and our experiences as Americans. Perhaps the Vietnam War and the other tragedies of the sixties have encouraged us to look back at the Western past and the whole of American history with an eye to understanding the whys of Vietnam and showing how it is not an aberration of our character, but possibly a side of it which we always knew was there but never wanted to admit. Westerns like *The Culpepper Cattle Co.* and *The Great Northfield, Minnesota Raid* purport to show the West as it really was—dirty and violent. *Butch Cassidy and the Sundance Kid* put the fifties themes of "too many Wringles" and the not-so-easy life of the outlaw together in a vision of a West being closed by "those guys" who work for the railroad. The question of *Butch Cassidy*—"who are those guys?"—could well stand as the epitaph for the sixties. Who are those guys who seem to be threatening our country, our ideals, our way of life? Who led us into a disastrous war? Who mysteriously killed off the major figures of an era—John and Robert Kennedy, Malcolm X, Martin Luther King, Medgar Evers, Chaney, Schwerner, and Goodman, Jeffrey Miller and Allison Krause and the thousands who have come home from Nam in metal boxes? In films like *Butch Cassidy* the question is often raised, but usually only briefly answered. In *Pat Garrett and Billy the Kid* and other films by Sam Peckinpah, as well as in the movies of other directors, notably Robert Altman and Monte Hellman, an answer to the question is suggested.

The Peckinpah, Hellman, Altman Westerns can be said to be an extension of those of the fifties in that they too are committed to exploring and showing the complexities and ambiguities of the Western and of America in terms of dialogue, plot, and theme. They deemphasize action and stunting, although in different degrees. Hellman's Westerns are virtually devoid of stunting and action, focusing on the suspense of the quest or the escape. *The Wild Bunch*, on the other hand, has a great deal of stunning violent action, from its opening image of the

scorpions and the ants to the final bloody climax. In fact *The B* probably contains a great deal more action than any of the se fifties Westerns. Lest I be caught in a trap of my own making I say that *The Wild Bunch* utilizes action for the purpose of and plot rather than vice versa as in earlier Westerns. In this is closer to the fifties Westerns.

Peckinpah's use of what amounts to a whole series of violer sequences suggests to me several ways in which he, Hellman, man differ from their fifties predecessors. The first and mo tant difference is that these three directors confront Ameri Western head-on, whereas the directors of the fifties see snipping around the edges. To me the archetypal fifties *Shane*, with that final sequence suggesting that the whol very well have been a small boy's dream. To Peckinpah whole thing is anything but a dream, although at times nightmare.

What they suggest is that the simple polarities of V America—the good versus evil, frontier versus city, ci barbarism values which John Cawelti alludes to in I fining the Western—are not polarities but are intima America with its puritanical conscience is both drea That such events as Vietnam and World War II fl basic urges. As Kitses was moved to say, *"The Wi* ica." [2] This leads to another characteristic use of t directors—to suggest parallels with contemporary ern has always, to some extent, related past to example, in many of the Westerns made durin villain is a banker or a businessman. One coul study of Western villains, equating them with Certainly, like all art, the Western cannot hel which is creating it; while some of this may be banker, some may not. What Peckinpah, H to this aspect of the Western is a complex rary conflicts, figures, etc. (like the banker) tween these elements and the Western itse an indictment of the implicit militarism society, but he is also related to the Wild outlawry of Mapache grows out of a sir the Bunch. Fittingly, the first scene of the disguised as soldiers in order to rob a ba "[He] is deeply rooted in, and like his can past. . . . And it is this tension w tive allegorical quality, the present ig

[2] Jim Kitses, *Horizons West*. Bloomingt 1969, p. 168.

and it is Ford, especially the later Ford of *Liberty Valance* and *Cheyenne Autumn,* whom Peckinpah most resembles in his thematic use of the idea of open options. In these late Ford films the open options of *My Darling Clementine,* which suggested an optimism for the future, become increasingly dark and pessimistic. In *Liberty Valance* it is the politician and all he represents who is a false hero to society, while the real Westerner dies in a pauper's grave, unrewarded for the deed which has become another man's road to glory.

Where Ford uses the symbol of the cactus rose in *Liberty Valance* as a symbol for open options, Peckinpah uses the symbol of the automobile. For Ford the cactus rose is a positive symbol, suggesting an almost nostalgic longing for the world of the past, of the desert.[5] Peckinpah's use of the automobile suggests one aspect of how he differs from Ford. In *Cable Hogue* the hero is run over by an automobile in a tragicomic death scene that is the climax of the film. In *The Wild Bunch* (1968) the automobile is the prize possession of Mapache, the new breed of outlaw who is army, government, and criminal, and is used to drag Angel—who personifies in many ways the naïve, socialistic vision of Tom Joad in Ford's *Grapes of Wrath*—to an ugly and gruesome death. In Peckinpah's Westerns open options, whether they be the individualistic entrepreneurial vision of Cable Hogue or the communitarian, socialistic one of Angel or the more violent and ambiguous visions of the Wild Bunch and Judd and Westrum of *Ride the High Country,* are all smashed, with the positive ones being fittingly smashed by the automobile. In Ford, however, there is no smashing. The West passes with a whimper, quietly and out of sight, not with a bang. If Ford is nostalgic—with all the possibilities that suggests (for is nostalgia not an attempt to bring the past into the present?)—Peckinpah is darkly realistic, pessimistic.

What Peckinpah does with the idea of open options is to suspend it on a razor's edge, at that precise moment when Turner's historic frontier was closing. It is said that the guillotine makes a whooshing sound before one hears the thud of death. Peckinpah's Westerns have a whoosh to them that makes the thud at the falling of the razor resound throughout our identities as Americans.

In Altman there is no thud, no whoosh. Rather there is only the disturbing sense that the options never really were or really are as open as we and our myths would have them. In keeping with a kind of weird masochistic debunking that the movie establishment seems to be flaunting these days, *McCabe and Mrs. Miller* (1971) was advertised as a picture which finally shows The West as it really was, as if anyone—

---

[5] Ford's West is not the garden but the desert, the cactus rose. It is full of primitive savagery as well as beauty (another tie to Peckinpah). As Hallie points out in *Liberty Valance,* the untamed West has changed almost into a garden, or in the description of Lucy Mallory in *Stagecoach* as "an angel in a jungle."

especially the ad men—could separate myth and reality in the Western. Certainly there are no John Waynes here. The hero is a dumb gambler with a tongue gifted with picturesque swearing and the heroine is a frizzy-haired whore. McCabe runs around playing the sophisticate with his bowler hat and cigars, uttering the phrase, "If a frog had wings he wouldn't bump his ass so much"—a phrase that might serve as an epitaph for McCabe and an epigraph for the picture.

It is the ending of *McCabe* that is most suggestive of Altman's idea of open options, for it is an ending full of irony and references to similar endings in other Westerns. Most explicitly it seems a direct commentary on both the apocalpytic endings of Peckinpah and other sixties directors and the ending of a fifties "serious" Western, *High Noon*. McCabe, like Gary Cooper, finds himself facing three killers in an empty town. One by one he kills them all, only to freeze in the snow outside the door to Mrs. Miller's house. Mrs. Miller, unlike the heroine in *High Noon*, does not come to the aid of the hero, but rather is shown at the end of the picture zonked out on opium. The town? The town of Presbyterian Church wants no part of McCabe's fight. In a beautiful bit of visual irony the town is shown putting out the fire in the church while McCabe struggles to put out the fire in Presbyterian Church. The town may have a sense of oneness and community but it is a oneness that might exist whether McCabe or the mining monopoly controlled it. It fights to save a building when it might have fought to save a human being. If a frog had wings he wouldn't bump his ass so much. The point is we are all frogs, we do not have wings, and we bump our asses a lot.

For McCabe, for Altman, there are no open options. Presbyterian Church is at the opening a small, dirty town where men get drunk, play cards, and occasionally kill each other. At the close it is a bigger, cleaner town perhaps destined to be a company town, but it is still a town where men get drunk, play cards, and occasionally kill each other. Even Peckinpah's apocalyptic ending is denied McCabe. He ends with a whimper, not with a bang. There is no whoosh, no thud. Only the wind blowing the snow over the town. The sameness of the seasons, of the town, of man. There are no open options, only options, and those are frighteningly limited by what one is and by circumstances.

Hellman, on the other hand, brings an existentialist hope to the idea. His philosophical twist to the idea of open options is an interesting one. What he suggests is that the West is so open that its options are also closed. This paradox may best be explained by reference to Sartre's play *No Exit*, to which *The Shooting* (1965) is a direct parallel. In *No Exit* a group of characters sit around a room trying to decide who they are, how they got there, and, ultimately, how to get out. The irony is that they could all get out if they just got up and walked out.

The Shooting takes place in a dimensionless space that in many ways is parallel to Sartre's room. In this wall-less room a man is engaged by a woman to track down the mysterious man who killed her baby. Just as in *No Exit*, clues are dropped as to the identity of the man, and also as in *No Exit* the man is constantly faced with the choice of staying in the room or leaving. At the end the hero makes his decision, only to find the man he has been tracking is his look-alike brother. In *Ride in the Whirlwind* (1965) Hellman uses the open-options idea to create an atmosphere of paranoia. Accepting with reservation an invitation to share grub and a campsite with some outlaws, three down-on-their-luck cowboys are caught up in a posse's ambush. Two of the three escape and the remainder of the picture deals with their attempt to elude the relentlessly pursuing posse of vigilantes. What is both complex and optimistic about Hellman's open options is the existentialist twist he gives them. In Hellman's Westerns past and present become fused in a series of questions about what, why, where, when, how. Hellman, like other existentialists, would have it that we are all historians, that history is what we make of the past and what we do *now*. Ultimately Hellman, like Sartre and Camus, suggests that even if the options are frighteningly narrow we can still try to decide where, when, and how we will die. Yet even here fate may intervene and we may not succeed.

In *Pat Garrett and Billy the Kid* Peckinpah takes the earlier open-options themes of *Cable Hogue* and *The Wild Bunch* and shows them not as related themes but as warring opposites. Where Hogue and the businessman, the Bunch and Mapache seem related to one another, Pat and Billy no longer are. Pat has sold out to the establishment, to big business and big government, which threaten Billy and the open options of the less powerful, like the Mexicans. *Pat and Billy* is almost a return to the earlier Western cycle of good guys versus bad guys, the individual versus the big rancher—I say "almost" because the so-called hero gets wiped out in the end.

But is Billy really the hero and might we not possibly draw a message of hope from this Peckinpah Western which does not exist in the others? The answer to both questions is Yes and that Yes is wrapped up in Dylan's character, Alias. Alias, not Billy, is the center of the film, with his name connoting his role as a sort of everyman and yet no man. In *The Odyssey*, Odysseus is asked by the Cyclops what his name is and he replies, "No Man." Dylan's Alias suggests a similar answer for a modern man plagued by closing options. The answer to fighting these forces is not mindless protest, or the violent resistance of the Bunch or Billy, or even the ignorance of a Hogue. Alias fights the establishment, but he fights it with stealth and cunning on his own terms. Note that in the movie Alias never uses a gun, and that when he uses his knife it is totally unexpected. Alias/Dylan—as I've said it is difficult to separate their roles—is also a newspaperman/writer. Like Odysseus he can trick Cyclops with words.

Alias, like Cain, the hero of the TV Western *Kung Fu,* is operating out of a different set of values from that of his opponents. Alias, like Cain, seems to suggest that perhaps a new Western, new values, and a new America is surfacing.

The emergence of the tip of that new vision is another Western, *Jeremiah Johnson* (1972). *Jeremiah Johnson* may well be called the first ecological Western, for ecology in the deepest sense of the word is the main theme of the movie. In the struggles of the mountain man Jeremiah Johnson with the mountains, weather, and Indians we see an image of ourselves and our own relations with the environment, all captured with a brilliant photography that for once is not mere window dressing.

The plot of the movie is like a Greek tragedy, with omens unheeded and the flaw of character leading to the death of Johnson's family. There is also a great deal of the American Indians' world view contained in the movie, and obviously someone did a great deal of reading on Indians, as is evidenced by the authentic costuming and the inclusion of a scene in which a cornered brave sings his death chant—the first time I know of that a Western has included it.

Johnson as a tragic figure is one whose soul is disputed over by two forces—the settlers and the Indians. The settlers symbolize progress, "civilization," taming the land as opposed to the Indians' preference for living with the land. Only one white man understands this, the old trapper Griz, who hunts grizzly bear in clothes of animal skins while living out of a house that seems a part of the mountain. The other whites—the cavalry, the settlers, other trappers—do not. *Jeremiah Johnson*'s settlers seem direct slaps at John Ford and the Ford vision, from the image of the cavalry to the mad settler woman singing "Shall We Gather at the River" by the tombstones of her family. Johnson seems to opt for the settlers, building an outlandish log cabin that in no way resembles Griz's, then offering to guide the cavalry through forbidden ground to rescue a stranded wagon train.

It is only at the end of the film that Johnson comes to the understanding that has eluded him. Fittingly, he is shown clothed in furs and, fittingly, his understanding is symbolized by an Indian's upraised hand. Like the trapper Griz he will build a house that is part of the mountain rather than the home he had built for his family, or like the homes of the settlers killed by the Indians all of which required that the land be cleared. He will live with nature, as the Indians do, not against it, as do the settlers. Hopefully we will also learn that lesson before it is too late.

Seventy Years on the Trail:
A Selected Chronology
of the Western Movie

1903   Edwin S. Porter's *The Great Train Robbery*, the first narrative Western.

1908   D. W. Griffith begins to make occasional one-reel Westerns for Biograph.

       G. M. Anderson begins Western production with *The Bandit Makes Good*, buys screen rights to the Peter B. Kyne character, "Broncho Billy," and becomes the first Western star.

1910   Harry Carey begins making one-reel Westerns.

1911   D. W. Griffith's *Fighting Blood*. A one-reeler featuring a spectacular Indian attack.

       Thomas H. Ince, next to Griffith the most talented producer-director of the early film era, begins to make Westerns.

1913   Cecil B. DeMille's *The Squaw Man* with Dustin Farnum. DeMille's first film and the first feature-length Western.

       D. W. Griffith's *The Battle at Elderbusch Gulch* with Lillian Gish. The best of Griffith's surviving Westerns.

1914   Cecil B. DeMille's *The Virginian* with Dustin Farnum. The first film version of Owen Wister's famous novel.

       The Spoilers. An early feature-length Western based on the novel by Rex Beach. The first of five versions of this film, all famous for their climactic fistfight.

       William S. Hart enters the movies and makes his first Western feature, *The Bargain*.

1916   *Hell's Hinges.* A William S. Hart feature-length Western with strong religious-allegorical overtones.

       Liberty, A Daughter of the U. S. A. The first Western serial.

1917   The greatest of Western directors, John Ford, begins to direct movies.

During this year he directs his first Western, *The Tornado,* and his first feature-length Western, *Straight Shooting,* with Harry Carey.

Tom Mix, who earlier had made unimportant short Westerns for William Selig, signs with Fox and soon becomes the most popular Western hero of the silent movies.

1919   Buck Jones becomes a Western star for Fox in *The Last Straw.*

Hoot Gibson begins a series of two-reelers for Universal and brings an element of humor into his portrayal of the Western hero. Until 1923, most of Hoot's two-reelers were directed by John Ford.

1920   Fred Niblo's *The Mark of Zorro.* Douglas Fairbanks stars in the first movie about the masked hero of Old California.

Maurice Tourneur's *The Last of the Mohicans.* A lavishly filmed version of James Fenimore Cooper's classic.

William S. Hart's biggest box-office success, *The Toll Gate.*

1921   Hoot Gibson makes his first Western feature for Universal, *Action,* directed by John Ford.

1923   James Cruze's *The Covered Wagon,* the first "epic" Western. A film largely responsible for making Westerns permanently popular: the year after *The Covered Wagon,* studio production of Westerns tripled.

William S. Hart plays a highly romanticized *Wild Bill Hickok.*

1924   Irving Willat's *Wanderer of the Wasteland* with Jack Holt and Billie Dove. The first feature-length film to be shot entirely in color (two-color technicolor). Based on the novel by Zane Grey.

John Ford's *The Iron Horse* with George O'Brien. The silent movies' most lavish attempt to tell the story about the building of the first transcontinental railroad.

Ken Maynard begins starring in his first series of Westerns.

1925   Buster Keaton parodies the Western in *Go West.*

Gary Cooper appears as an extra in his first Western, *The Lucky Horseshoe,* starring Tom Mix.

Tom Mix stars in a movie version of Zane Grey's first bestselling Western novel, *Riders of the Purple Sage.*

William S. Hart's last Western, *Tumbleweeds,* includes one of the best spectacle scenes of the silent screen, the Cherokee Strip land-rush sequence.

1926   Colonel Tim McCoy becomes a Western star for MGM.

John Ford's *3 Bad Men* includes a spectacular recreation of the 1876 Dakota land rush.

1927   George B. Seitz' *The Vanishing American* with Richard Dix. A well-intentioned but ultimately patronizing tribute to the American Indian. Based on the novel by Zane Grey.

The Great K and A Train Robbery. The best silent Tom Mix movie still in circulation.

The Red Raiders features some extraordinary trick riding by Ken Maynard.

1928   The mechanical problems of using the new sound equipment outdoors brings about a temporary decline in the popularity of Western movies. Fred Thomson, one of the most popular Western stars of the 1920's, dies of an illness at the height of his popularity.

1929   Raoul Walsh's *In Old Arizona* becomes a successful sound film and renews commercial interest in the Western. An Academy Award to Warner Baxter for his portrayal of the Cisco Kid.

Victor Fleming's *The Virginian.* Gary Cooper stars in this first sound version.

1930   King Vidor's *Billy the Kid* with Johnny Mack Brown. The first major sound-film biography of the legendary New Mexico outlaw.

Raoul Walsh's "epic" Western, *The Big Trail,* marks the starring debut of John Wayne. The failure of this film at the box office relegates Wayne to cheap B Westerns throughout the 1930's.

1931   Randolph Scott achieves Western stardom in *Lone Cowboy.*

Wesley Ruggles' *Cimarron* with Richard Dix and Irene Dunne. The only Western ever to receive an Academy Award as best picture of the year.

1932   *Destry Rides Again.* Tom Mix's first sound Western. Based on the novel by Max Brand.

Edward Cahn's *Law and Order* with Walter Houston. An early sound-film treatment of the Gunfight at the OK Corral legend.

1933   Henry Hathaway's *The Thundering Herd* with Harry Carey. Based on Zane Grey's attempt at an epic novel about the hunting of the buffalo.

The Strawberry Roan with Ken Maynard. The first Western to be built around a popular song.

1934   Howard Hawks' and Jack Conway's *Viva Villa* with Wallace Beery as the violent but lovable bandit-patriot.

1935   Gene Autry stars in a Western with music, *Tumbling Tumbleweeds,* and quickly becomes the most popular of the singing cowboys.

Tom Mix makes his last movie, a fifteen-chapter serial, *The Miracle Rider,* for Mascot Pictures.

Mascot Films, Monogram Pictures and several other small film companies merge to form Republic Pictures Corporation, the most notable producer of quality B Westerns.

Powdersmoke Range with the "Three Mesquiteers" (Harry Carey, Hoot Gibson, "Big Boy" Williams) initiates the popular B Western "trio" concept for featuring Western heroes.

William Boyd appears in the first of the long running "Hopalong Cassidy" series, *Hop-A-Long Cassidy*.

1936   Cecil B. DeMille's *The Plainsman* with Cary Cooper and Jean Arthur. A big-scale attempt to recreate the Wild Bill Hickok–Calamity Jane legend.

James Cruze's *Sutter's Gold*. A clumsy attempt to tell the story of the discovery of gold in California.

King Vidor's *The Texas Rangers*, a spectacular Western supposedly based on Rangers' records.

1937   Frank Lloyd's *Wells Fargo* features Joel McCrea in his first major Western.

1938   The Lone Ranger comes from the radio to the movies in a Republic serial, *The Lone Ranger*.

Roy Rogers begins to make "singing cowboy" Westerns at Republic Pictures.

1939   Cecil B. DeMille's *Union Pacific* with Joel McCrea. A mammoth attempt to tell the story of the building of the transcontinental railroad.

Henry King's *Jesse James*, the most ambitious treatment of the James legend, with Henry Fonda as Frank and Tyrone Power as Jesse.

George Marshall's *Destry Rides Again* with James Stewart and Marlene Dietrich. The best known "comic" Western of the 1930's.

Michael Curtiz' *Dodge City*. Errol Flynn's first Western.

Stagecoach. John Ford's most famous Western. Rescued John Wayne from the B-picture grind and made him a topflight star. First of the many Westerns Ford filmed in Monument Valley. An Academy Award to Thomas Mitchell for his role as the lovable drunkard, Doc Boone.

William S. Hart's *Tumbleweeds* is re-released with an added sound prologue in which the sixty-nine-year-old Hart gives a touching farewell to his audience.

1940   German director Fritz Lang makes his first American Western, *The Return of Frank James*, a sequel to the 1939 *Jesse James*.

Rouben Mamoulian's *The Mark of Zorro* with Tyrone Power. An entertaining remake of the 1920 original.

William Wyler's *The Westerner* with Gary Cooper. An Academy Award to Walter Brennan for his portrayal of Judge Roy Bean.

1941   David Miller's *Billy the Kid* with Robert Taylor. A technicolor version of Billy's life and death.

Fritz Lang's *Western Union* with Randolph Scott and Robert Young. A romantic dramatization of stringing the telegraph lines in the West. Only loosely based on the Zane Grey novel of the same name.

Raoul Walsh's *They Died With Their Boots On* with Errol Flynn as a whitewashed General George Armstrong Custer leading his men to heroic deaths.

1942 Buck Jones dies in the Coconut Grove fire while heroically helping others to safety.

1943 Howard Hughes' *The Outlaw*, with superbuxom Jane Russell, creates a market for the "sexy" Western.

William Wellman's *The Ox-Bow Incident*, with Henry Fonda, questions the validity of violent western justice.

1944 William Wellman's *Buffalo Bill*, with Joel McCrea as the legendary Cody in a highly romanticized film biography.

1945 Stuart Heisler's *Along Came Jones*. A comedy Western in which Gary Cooper parodies his own silent cowboy image.

1946 John Ford's *My Darling Clementine* with Henry Fonda as Wyatt Earp and Victor Mature as Doc Holiday. The best of the Wyatt Earp-OK Corral movies.

1947 King Vidor's *Duel in the Sun* with Jennifer Jones and Gregory Peck. The most lavishly produced of all the "sexy" Westerns.

1948 *Fort Apache* with John Wayne and Henry Fonda. The first of John Ford's U. S. Cavalry trilogy.

Howard Hawks' *Red River* with John Wayne and Montgomery Clift. The best cattle-drive Western.

Leslie Fenton's *Whispering Smith*. Alan Ladd's first starring role in a Western.

Treasure of the Sierra Madre with Humphrey Bogart and Tim Holt. A morality tale about the evils of a lust for gold. An Academy Award to John Huston as best director and to his father, Walter Huston, as best supporting actor.

The Hopalong Cassidy Westerns go on TV and re-establish Hoppy's popularity.

1949 John Ford's *Three Godfathers* with John Wayne and Harry Carey, Jr. A remake of Ford's 1919 feature, *Marked Men*, and dedicated to the star of *Marked Men*, Harry Carey.

I Shot Jesse James. The first movie by the respected action director Samuel Fuller.

Raoul Walsh's *Colorado Territory* with Joel McCrea. An interesting combination of two popular non-Westerns, *Odd Man Out* and *High Sierra*.

She Wore A Yellow Ribbon with John Wayne and Ben Johnson. The second (and best) of John Ford's U. S. Cavalry trilogy.

1950 Anthony Mann's *Winchester 73*. The first movie in the successful series of Westerns directed by Mann and starring James Stewart.

Delmer Daves' *Broken Arrow* with James Stewart. Begins a trend in Westerns for a more sympathetic portrayal of the Indians.

Henry King's *The Gunfighter* with Gregory Peck. Begins a trend in the fifties for Westerns featuring the weary, loner-gunfighter.

John Ford's *Rio Grande* with John Wayne. The third of Ford's U. S. Cavalry trilogy.

Wagonmaster. John Ford's personal favorite of all his Westerns. Ben Johnson's finest starring role.

World War II hero Audie Murphy begins his career as a star of low-budget Westerns playing Billy the Kid in *The Kid From Texas.*

1952   *Bend of the River.* Anthony Mann adds lavish color landscapes to his series of Westerns with James Stewart.

Fred Zinnemann's *High Noon* begins a trend for "suspense" Westerns. An Academy Award for Gary Cooper.

Nicholas Ray's *The Lusty Men* with Arthur Kennedy and Robert Mitchum. Interesting depiction of rivalries between riders on the rodeo circuit.

1953   George Stevens' *Shane* portrays the gunfighter as a frontier Messiah. Alan Ladd as Shane. Also with Van Heflin, Jean Arthur and Brandon DeWilde as the child through whose eyes we see the story. Based on the novel by Jack Schaefer.

John Fallon's *Hondo* with John Wayne in the title role. The best of the 3-D Westerns.

1954   Nicholas Ray's *Johnny Guitar* with Joan Crawford. Voted the best Western ever made in a poll of French film critics.

Robert Aldrich's *Vera Cruz* with Gary Cooper and Burt Lancaster. One of the earliest and best Westerns on the theme of has-been gunfighters doing one more job.

Television finishes its destruction of the cheap Saturday matinee Western. *Two Guns and A Badge* with Wayne Morris is the last B Western.

1955   *Davy Crockett, King of the Wild Frontier* with Fess Parker and Buddy Ebsen. Walt Disney's famous TV trilogy is edited and released as a movie.

Jacques Tourneur's *Wichita,* with Joel McCrea as Wyatt Earp in his early lawman days.

John Sturges' *Bad Day at Black Rock* with Spencer Tracy. A contemporary Western dealing in part with American guilt over the treatment of the Japanese during World War II.

King Vidor's *Man Without a Star* with Kirk Douglas. An interesting study of the effects of barbed wire on a free-and-easy cowboy.

Raoul Walsh's *The Tall Men* with Clark Gable. A lavishly produced cattle-drive Western.

1956   Columbia Pictures' *Blazing the Overland Trail.* The last Western serial made in the U. S.

John Ford's *The Searchers.* An excellent rescue-of-the-white-captive-from-the-Indians Western. John Wayne's favorite Western role.

Richard Brooks' *The Last Hunt* with Robert Taylor and Arthur Kennedy. Offbeat Western depicting the final slaughter of the buffalo.

Seven Men From Now. The first of six excellent low-budget Westerns starring Randolph Scott and directed by Bud Boetticher.

Samuel Fuller's *Run of the Arrow* with Rod Steiger. Indian culture is shown to be a valid alternative to white culture.

1957   Delmer Daves' *3:10 To Yuma* with Glenn Ford, one of the best suspense Westerns made after *High Noon.*

1958   Anthony Mann's *Man of the West.* Gary Cooper's last Western and one of his best.

Arthur Penn's *The Left-Handed Gun* with Paul Newman. A psychological Western based on the life of Billy the Kid.

Henry Hathaway's *From Hell To Texas* with Don Murray. A sprawling chase Western which uses the wide CinemaScope screen with particular effectiveness.

William Wyler's *The Big Country* with Gregory Peck. An overproduced story of feuding cattle barons. An Academy Award to Burl Ives.

1959   Howard Hawks' *Rio Bravo* with John Wayne and Dean Martin. Hawks' most critically praised Western.

1960   *Comanche Station.* The last of the Bud Boetticher-Randolph Scott Westerns.

Don Siegel's *Flaming Star.* The best Elvis Presley movie.

John Sturges' *The Magnificent Seven* with Yul Brynner and Steve McQueen. Based on Akira Kurosawa's Japanese classic, *The Seven Samurai.*

John Wayne directs and stars in an epic, *The Alamo.*

1961   *The Deadly Companions* with Brian Keith and Maureen O'Hara. The first movie Western by director Sam Peckinpah.

John Huston's *The Misfits.* A contemporary Western which includes the final screen performances of Clark Gable and Marilyn Monroe.

Marlon Brando tries his hand at directing in *One-Eyed Jacks,* with Brando and Karl Malden.

1962   Three excellent Westerns all based on a feeling of loss for the vanishing West.

David Miller's *Lonely Are the Brave* with Kirk Douglas.

John Ford's *The Man Who Shot Liberty Valance* with James Stewart, John Wayne and Lee Marvin.

Sam Peckinpah's *Ride the High Country*. Randolph Scott's last Western. Also starring Joel McCrea.

1963   *How the West Was Won*. The first cinerama Western. Directed by John Ford, Henry Hathaway and George Marshall.

Martin Ritt's *Hud* with Paul Newman as a contemporary Western antihero. An Academy Award for Melvyn Douglas.

1964   John Ford's *Cheyenne Autumn*. Ford's last Western.

Sam Peckinpah's *Major Dundee* with Charlton Heston. A classic example of how studio editing can destroy the artistic intentions of a director.

1965   Eliot Silverstein's *Cat Ballou*. An Academy Award for Lee Marvin for his dual role as a nasty villain and a drunken hero.

1966   Richard Brooks' *The Professionals,* with Lee Marvin and Burt Lancaster, makes a mockery of the idealistic quest theme in Westerns.

1967   Burt Kennedy's *Welcome to Hard Times* with Henry Fonda. An intentionally allegorical Western.

John Sturges' *Hour of the Gun* with Jason Robards as Doc Holiday and James Garner as Wyatt Earp. The most accurate filmed retelling of the Gunfight at the OK Corral.

Martin Ritt's *Hombre* with Paul Newman. A calling into question of the idealism of John Ford's *Stagecoach*.

Sergio Leone's ritualistically violent movie *A Fistful of Dollars* is released in the United States and establishes a market for "Spaghetti Westerns." Clint Eastwood's portrayal of "the man with no name" makes him an international star.

Sergio Leone's *The Good, The Bad, and The Ugly*. A cynical three-hour Western epic with Clint Eastwood (good), Lee Van Cleef (bad), and Eli Wallach (ugly).

1968   Sidney Pollack's *The Scalphunters* with Burt Lancaster and Ossie Davis. An entertaining action Western and at the same time a serious statement about the relationships between blacks, whites and Indians.

Ted Post's *Hang 'Em High* with Clint Eastwood. The Western becomes a vehicle for an unusually literate discussion of capital punishment.

Tom Gries' *Will Penny* with Charlton Heston. An attempt to realistically portray the life of a veteran cowboy.

1969   George Roy Hill's *Butch Cassidy and the Sundance Kid* with Paul Newman as Butch and Robert Redford as the Kid. The top-grossing Western of all time—nearly thirty million dollars.

John Wayne parodies himself in Henry Hathaway's *True Grit* and wins his first Academy Award.

Sam Peckinpah's *The Wild Bunch* with William Holden and Ernest

Borgnine. The bloodiest American Western made to that time and one of the best.

Sergio Leone's *Once Upon A Time in the West* with Henry Fonda and Charles Bronson. An epic centering around the building of a railroad.

1970   Andrew V. McLaglen's *Chisum* has John Wayne as one of the major adversaries in a historically inaccurate depiction of the famed Lincoln County War.

Ralph Nelson's *Soldier Blue,* with Candice Bergen, clumsily rejects the heroic U. S. Cavalry image of the John Ford Westerns and turns the Cavalry into bestial murderers in a reconstruction of the infamous Sand Creek Massacre.

William Fraker's *Monte Walsh* with Lee Marvin and Jeanne Moreau. A successful recreation of the mood of the paintings and drawings of Charles Russell.

1971   Arthur Penn's *Little Big Man* with Dustin Hoffman depicts Indian culture as more honorable and dignified than the white man's and contends that General Custer was a madman.

John Wayne passes the legacy of the Western hero down to eleven young boys in Mark Rydell's *The Cowboys.*

Peter Fonda's *The Hired Hand* with Fonda and Warren Oates. A touching examination of the conflict between home and freedom.

Robert Altman's *McCabe and Mrs. Miller,* with Julie Christie and Warren Beatty, lyrically recreates the Washington frontier of 1903 with striking color photography by cinematographer Vilmos Zsigmond.

Tom Laughlin's *Billy Jack* with Laughlin and Delores Taylor places the traditional Western hero in a morally complex contemporary setting.

1972   Philip Kaufman's *The Great Northfield Minnesota Raid,* with Cliff Robertson and Robert Duval, creates a comedy out of the exploits of the James Gang and makes a folk hero of Cole Younger.

Sidney Poitier's *Buck and the Preacher* with Poitier and Harry Belafonte. The first major Western to feature black heroes.

Sidney Pollack's *Jeremiah Johnson,* with Robert Redford, gives the movies its first mountain-man folk hero.

1973   Clint Eastwood's *High Plains Drifter,* with Eastwood, makes the Western hero an instrument of Old Testament-like justice.

Sam Peckinpah's *Pat Garrett and Billy the Kid* with Kris Kristofferson and James Coburn makes Billy a heroic alternative to the growing loss of individuality in the last days of the old West.

Selected Bibliography

Books

Balshofer, Fred J. and Arthur C. Miller. *One Reel A Week*. Berkeley: California: University of California Press, 1967. The memoirs of two pioneer film makers, which include reminiscences about many early Westerns.

Barbour, Alan G. *The Thrill of It All*. New York: Collier Books, 1971. Brief descriptions of various categories of "B" Westerns. Mostly photos.

Bazin, André. *What Is Cinema?* VOLUME II, trans. Hugh Gray. Berkeley, California: University of California Press, 1971. Includes translations of three of Bazin's best known essays on Westerns: "The Western, or the American Film par excellence"; "The Evolution of the Western"; and "The Outlaw."

Bichard, Robert S. *The Western in the 1920's*. Available only at Charles K. Feldman Library, AFI Center for Advanced Film Studies, Beverly Hills, California. Interviews with seven people active in Western film production in the 1920's including Hoot Gibson, Ann Little and Irvin Willat.

* Cawelti, John G. *The Six-Gun Mystique*. Bowling Green, Ohio: Bowling Green University Popular Press, 1971. Includes an excellent article on the Western formula, selected bibliography and lists of major Western films and directors.

Corneau, Ernest N. *The Hall of Fame of Western Film Stars*. North Quincy, Massachusetts: Christopher Publishing House, 1969. Short biographical sketches of 150 Western film personalities. Includes lists of performers' films but lacks dates of release.

Everson, William K. *The Bad Guys*. New York: Citadel Press, 1964. Includes a chapter on actors best known for their roles as Western outlaws.

————. *A Pictorial History of the Western Film*. New York: Citadel Press, 1969. Mainly a shortened version of the materials in Fenin and Everson's *The Western From Silents to Cinerama*. Discusses materials through the 1960's. Heavily illustrated.

Eyles, Allen. *The Western: An Illustrated Guide*. New York: A. S. Barnes and Co., 1967. A reference with annotations of 358 actors, fictional characters, directors, etc. Includes a title index.

Fenin, George N. and William K. Everson. *The Western From Silents to Cinerama*. New York: Orion Press, 1962. Despite some factual errors and an insistence on judging all Westerns on the basis of William S. Hart "realism," this book, because of its comprehensive breadth and detail, remains the single best historical study of the genre. Beautifully illustrated.

―――. *The Western: From Silents to The Seventies*. New York: Grossman Publishers, 1973. An altogether welcome updating of *The Western: From Silents to Cinerama*.

Friar, Ralph and Natasha Friar. *The Only Good Indian . . . The Hollywood Gospel*. New York: Drama Book Specialists/Publishers, 1972. A history of the distortion of Indian cultures in American movies. Good source material and illustrations but overall argument suffers from a lack of perspective. Includes useful subject listing of films.

* Kitses, Jim. *Horizons West*. Bloomington, Indiana: Indiana University Press, 1969. An excellent chapter on the nature of the Western genre and analyses of the Westerns of Anthony Mann, Bud Boetticher and Sam Peckinpah. Includes filmographies.

Lahue, Kalton C. *Winners of the West: The Sagebrush Heroes of the Silent Screen*. New York: A. S. Barnes and Co., 1970. Short, incomplete and often inaccurate profiles of thirty-eight Western stars. Overall tone tends toward condescension.

Manchel, Frank. *Cameras West*. Englewood Cliffs, New Jersey: Prentice-Hall, Inc., 1971. A short but readable and usually reliable history of Western movies. Includes several comparisons between historical Westerners and their movie counterparts.

McClure, Arthur F. and Ken D. Jones. *Heroes, Heavies, and Sagebrush*. New York: A. S. Barnes and Co., 1972. Short biographical sketches of familiar "B" Western performers. Brief, incomplete filmographies. Mostly illustrations.

Parkinson, Michael and Clyde Jeavons. *A Pictorial History of Westerns*. London, England: Hamlyn, 1972. Chapters on history, stars, directors, spaghetti Westerns, TV Westerns. Lavishly illustrated. Some stills in color.

Tuska, Jon. *100 Finest Westerns*. Garden City, New York: Doubleday & Co., Inc., 1975. Detailed analyses of Westerns from the earliest silents to the present.

Warman, Eric and Tom Vallance. *Westerns*. London, England: Golden Pleasure Books, 1964.

Articles

"Accuracy in Indian Subjects." *Moving Picture World*, V (July 10, 1909), 48. Westerns should be historically accurate, especially when dealing with Indian subjects.

Austen, David. "Continental Westerns." *Films and Filming*, XVII (July, 1971), 36–44. Relates the rise of the Continental Western to international popularity. Includes an alphabetical filmography of 172 Continental Westerns.

Barker, Warren J., M.D. "The Stereotyped Western Story: Its Latent Meaning and Psychoeconomic Function." *Psychoanalytic Quarterly*, XXIV (1955), 270–80.

Barr, Charles. "Western." *Axle Quarterly*, No. 3 (Spring, 1963), 13–17. The chief virtue of the Western is its simplicity. Its chief appeal is in its fulfilling of the audience's paradoxical need for both adventure and security. 1960's Westerns are becoming increasingly self-conscious.

Barsness, John A. "A Question of Standard." *Film Quarterly*, XXI:1 (Fall, 1967), 32–37. *High Noon* is the perfect mythic Western. *The Misfits* rejects the mythic idealism of the formula Western and attempts to dramatize the real.

Bartlett, Randolph. "Where Do We Go From Here?" *Photoplay*, XV (February, 1919), 36–37, 109. A brief history of Westerns from 1907–1919.

Batman, Richard Dale. "The Founding of the Motion Picture Industry." *Journal of the West*, X:4 (October, 1971), 609–23. Western movie production was an important factor in the development of Hollywood into America's center of film production.

Beale, L. "The American Way West." *Films and Filming*, XVIII:7 (April, 1972), 24–30. Westerns as American cultural heritage. The difference between "old" and "new" Westerns.

Bean, Robin. "Way Out West in Yugoslavia," *Films and Filming*, XI:12 (September, 1965), 49–51. A brief description of German Westerns and an interview with Stewart Granger, one of Germany's leading Western stars.

Blanchard, Phyllis. "The Child and the Motion Picture." In her *The Child and Society*. (New York: Longman, Green and Co., 1928), pp. 189–207. The early part of the article cites studies that show that the favorite genres of children attending silent movies were comedies and Westerns.

Bluestone, George. "The Changing Cowboy: From Dime Novel to Dollar Film." *Western Humanities Review*, XIV (Summer, 1960), 331–37. The development of Westerns from earliest dime novels to "adult" Western movies. The formula in 1950's Westerns broke down and the Western became more complex and ambiguous.

Boatright, Mody C. "The Cowboy Enters the Movies." In Hudson, Wilson M. and Allen Maxwell, ed. *The Sunny Slopes of Long Ago*. Pub. of Texas Folklore Society XXXIII (Dallas, Texas: Southern Methodist University Press, 1966), pp. 51–69. A description of the most common themes of Westerns, 1908–1912, based largely on the reading of story summaries from *Moving Picture World*. Most early Westerns lacked the formula predictability of later Westerns.

————. "The Formula in Cowboy Fiction and Drama." *Western Folklore*, XXVIII:2 (April, 1969), 136–45. The essentials of any formula Western and the seven plots that are used to meet them.

* Brauer, Ralph, "Who Are Those Guys? The Movie Western During the TV Era." *Journal of Popular Film*, II:4 (Fall, 1973). Westerns since the 1950's share the theme of "closing options."

Bush, W. Stephen. "Moving Picture Absurdities." *Moving Picture World*, IX (September 16, 1911), 773. A criticism of film producers for their unrealistic, stereotyped portrayals of the Indians.

Cawelti, John G. "The Gunfighter and Society." *The American West*, V (March, 1968), 30–35, 76–78. Early Westerns had external conflict and action whereas new "adult" Westerns have mainly internal conflict and action. Two standard "Adult" Western plot devices are "the man in the middle" and "group involvement."

———. "Prolegomena to the Western." *Studies in Public Communication*, IV (Autumn, 1962), 57–70. Suggestions for the proper study of Westerns Cawelti himself later employs in his *The Six-Gun Mystique*.

* ———. "Reflections on the New Western Films." *The University of Chicago Magazine* (January–February, 1973), 25–32. The old, unified Western formula has split into several new types but all of these share in common a pessimistic view of society and an obsession with the place of violence in it.

Croizier, Ralph C. "Beyond East and West: The American Western and Rise of the Chinese Swordplay Movie." *Journal of Popular Film*, I:3 (Summer, 1972), 229–43. The major similarities and differences using Ralph Willett's "The American Western: Myth and Anti-Myth" as the touchstone to describe the Western.

Dyer, Peter John. "A Man's World." *Films and Filming*, V:8 (May, 1959), 13–15, 32–33. A short history of Westerns to 1940. Also, describes the influence of Westerns on other film genres.

* Elkin, Frederick. "The Psychological Appeal of the Hollywood Western." *Journal of Educational Sociology*, XXIV (October, 1950), 72–86. The formula Western offers several psychological comforts to children and to rural adults.

Emery, F. E. "Psychological Effects of the Western Film: a Study in Television Viewing." *Human Relations*, XII:3 (1959), 195–232. A study of the psychological results of showing a Western, *The Lone Hand*, on television to a group of schoolboys reveals that Westerns bring about temporary feelings about the way youngsters view their environment but do not cause systematic changes in "aggressive drives."

Esselman, Kathryn C. "When the Cowboy Stopped Kissing His Horse." *Journal of Popular Culture*, VI:2 (Fall, 1972), 337–49. Movie Westerns thrived on "lone wolf" Westerns but, because of their series format, TV Westerns tend to be "communal" in nature.

Everson, William K. "Europe Produces Westerns Too." *Films in Review*, IV:2 (February, 1953), 74–79. A report of the growing popularity on the continent of European-made Westerns just as production of the American "B" Western was coming to an end.

Fenin, George N. "The Western—Old and New." *Film Culture* (May–June, 1956), 7–10. Postwar Westerns like *Shane, High Noon* and *Tribute To A Bad Man* offer hope that Westerns may achieve their potential as history and myth. Earlier "B" Westerns failed to achieve this potential.

Fenin, George N. and William K. Everson. "The European Western." *Film Culture*, XX (1959), 59–72. A country-by-country survey of non-American Westerns before they gained popularity in the United States in the later sixties.

* Folsom, James K. " 'Western' Themes and Western Films." *Western American Literature*, II:3 (Fall, 1967), 195–203. Westerns "do not so much yearn for an older, simpler life as attempt to set up an alternate standard of values to the often shabby ones of modern finance capitalism." Westerns are a primarily visual art form.

Franklin, Eliza. "Westerns, First and Lasting." *The Quarterly of Film, Radio and Television*, VII (1952–1953), 109–15. "The Western has had a well-rounded career—from success with audiences of all ages, to overwhelming success with children, back to success with all age groups."

Georgakas, Dan. "They Have Not Spoken: American Indians in Film." *Film Quarterly*, XXV:3 (Spring, 1972), 26–32. "New" treatments of Indians in *A Man Called Horse, Soldier Blue, Little Big Man* and *Tell Them Willie Boy Is Here* may be well intentioned but in reality "tell us very little about the Native Americans and even less about ourselves and our own history."

Godfrey, Lionel. "A Heretic's View of Westerns." *Films and Filming*, XIII (May, 1967), 14–18. A highly personal, minimally reasoned evaluation of some of the Westerns of the 1950's and early 1960's.

Gruber, Frank. In his *The Pulp Jungle*. (Los Angeles, California: Sherbourne Press, Inc., 1967), pp. 183–86. There are seven Western plots: the Union Pacific story, the ranch story, the revenge story, Custer's last stand, the outlaw story, the marshal story. All Westerns fit one of these story forms.

* Homans, Peter. "Puritanism Revisited: An Analysis of the Contemporary Screen Image Western." *Studies in Public Communication*, No. 3 (Summer, 1961), 73–84. The formula Western is a "puritan morality tale in which the savior-hero redeems the community from the temptations of the devil."

"Horse Opera." *Life*, XXI:15 (October 7, 1946), 93–99. A photo essay on the making of a Republic "B" Western programmer, *Rio Grande Raiders* with Sunset Carson.

Jacobson, Herbert L. "Cowboy, Pioneer and American Soldier." *Sight and Sound*, XXII (1953), 189–90. Westerns have helped keep alive a military spirit in America which allowed the United States to triumph in both world wars. Arguments are based on broad speculation.

Jowett, Garth S. "The Concept of History in American Produced Films: an Analysis of the Films Made in the Period 1950–1961." *Journal of Popular Culture*, III:4 (Spring, 1970), 799–813. Includes data showing that Westerns

comprise about one half of the historical films made during the 1950's. Briefly
attempts to explain why.

Kaminsky, Stuart M. "The Samurai Film and the Western." *Journal of
Popular Film*, I:4 (Fall, 1972), 312–24. Major Samurai motifs and conventions and how these differ from Westerns.

Kitchin, Lawrence. "Decline of the 'Western.'" *The Listener*, LXXVI
(July 14, 1966), 54–55, 57. A sketchy argument attempting to prove that "in
taking shelter in the western dream America . . . deluded herself."

Lyon, Peter. "The Wild, Wild West." *American Heritage*, XI:5 (August,
1960), 33–48. Over many major Western heroes and heroines, Wild Bill
Hickok, Calamity Jane, Jesse James, Belle Starr, Wyatt Earp, Bat Masterson
and Billy the Kid, "there hangs the stink of evil." The essay is in reality a
vicious attack on movie and TV Westerns for presenting historical characters inaccurately.

Markfield, Wallace. "The Inauthentic Western: Problems on the Prairie."
American Mercury, LXXV:345 (September, 1952), 82–86. The Western has
lost its old, pure action and is bogged down by second-rate moralizing and
social commentary. Article tends to be personal opinion rather than in-depth
analysis.

McArthur, Colin. "The Roots of the Western." *Cinema* (October, 1969),
11–13. Westerns reflect a major split in the American psyche between the
agrarian myth as defined by Frederick Jackson Turner and the reality of industrialism.

Miller, Alexander. "The 'Western'—A Theological Note." *Christian Century*, LXXIV (November 27, 1957), 1409–10. Westerns contain every theological theme "except the final theme, the deep and healing dimension of guilt
and grace."

Miller, D. "New Words on Old Westerns." *Focus on Film*, XI (Autumn,
1972), 27–37. A survey of Westerns between 1940–1957.

Munden, Kenneth J., M.D. "A Contribution to the Psychological Understanding of the Origin of the Cowboy and His Myth." *American Imago*, XV:2
(Summer, 1958), pp. 103–48. A Freudian interpretation of the formula Western based on a case study of an actual cowboy. The essay suffers from an
overly narrow conception of the Western formula.

* Nachbar, Jack. "A Bibliography of Published Materials on Western
Movies." *Journal of Popular Film*, II:4 (Fall, 1973).

* ———. "Riding Shotgun: The Scattered Formula in Contemporary Western Movies." *The Film Journal*, II:3 (September, 1973). The splitting apart
of the once-unified Western formula reflects the disunity in American life.

* ———. "Seventy Years on the Trail: A Selected Chronology of The Western Movie." *Journal of Popular Film*, II:1 (Winter, 1973), 75–83. An annotated list, in chronological order, of 150 important Westerns.

Nussbaum, Martin. "The 'Adult Western' as an American Art Form." *Folklore,* LXX (September, 1959), 460–67. Adult Westerns appeal to modern audiences because they are morally complex and admit to limits of rationality.

————. "Sociological Symbolism of the 'Adult Western.'" *Social Forces,* XXIX:1 (October, 1960), 25–28. Westerns are currently popular because of the attraction of an unusual locale, the unique Western hero, the hero's independence, contact with nature, a modern notion of the complexity of morality, and the use of the gun.

Packer, James S. "It Don't Hurt Much, Ma'am." *American Heritage,* XXII:2 (February, 1971), 66–69. Gunshot wounds in the real West were much more incapacitating than are shown in Western movies.

Rieupeyrout, Jean-Louis. "The Western: A Historical Genre." *Quarterly of Film, Radio and Television,* VII (1952), 116–28. The best Westerns are not mere fictions but are essentially accurate recreations of the essence of American historical events. Examples are *My Darling Clementine* and *Fort Apache.*

* Ross, T. J. "Fantasy and Form in the Western: From Hart to Peckinpah." *December,* XII:1 (Fall, 1970), 158–69. A series of astute observations about the genre, including an attack on some of the propositions of Fenin and Everson and Robert Warshow, and setting forth reasons for the violent nature of the Western hero.

Scheide, Frank. "Mythicized Gunfighters of the Old West." *The Velvet Light Trap,* No. 8 (1973), 29–33. A comparison between the real Wild Bill Hickok, James Brothers, Younger Brothers and Dalton Gang and their movie counterparts.

Schein, Harry. "The Olympian Cowboy." *American Scholar,* XXIV (Summer, 1955), 309–20. The repetition of the Western formula creates in the audience "a ritualistic passivity similar to that which one finds in a congregation at divine service." Shane is "a suffering god, whose noble and bitter fate it is to sacrifice himself for others."

Sisk, John P. "The Western Hero." *Commonweal,* LXVI (July 12, 1957), 367–69. The popularity of the strong, independent Western hero is due to the modern American's feelings of weakness and failure in a complex world.

Terraine, John. "End of the Trail." *Films and Filming,* III (July, 1957), 9, 30. Westerns have evolved through several phases: lone rider, cavalrymen, Indians and, most recently, anti-Westerns. Each area is covered only superficially.

* Tuska, Jon. "The American Western Cinema: 1903–Present." *Views and Reviews* (February, 1974). A historical overview emphasizing Western stars and men prominent in Western production.

"The Vogue of Western and Military Drama." *Moving Picture World,* IX (August 5, 1911), 271–72. Indians are idolized on the screen because they are no longer a threat.

Waldmeir, Joseph J. "The Cowboy, the Knight, and Popular Taste."

Southern Folklore Quarterly, XXII:3 (September, 1958), 113–20. "The Western hero has become a stock cowboy whose moral and ethical frame of reference is chivalric." This is clearly exemplified in the story of the Lone Ranger.

* Warshow, Robert. "The Westerner." In his *The Immediate Experience* (Garden City, New York: Doubleday & Co., 1962), pp. 135–54. The Western hero is a "man of leisure," the last gentleman who defends his honor with guns. Includes an explanation of the anti-Western.

Warner, A. "Western Heroes." *Films and Filming*, XVIII:5 (February, 1972), 34–40. A description of Westerns constructed around the best known heroes.

Weaver, John D. "Destry Rides Again, and Again, and Again." *Holiday*, XXXIV (August, 1963), 77–80, 91. A very readable and often informative but occasionally condescending history of Western movies.

"What is an American Subject." *The Moving Picture World* (January 22, 1910). Reprinted in Kauffmann, Stanley and Bruce Henstell, eds. *American Film Criticism: From the Beginnings to 'Citizen Kane'* (New York: Liveright, 1972), pp. 35–37. Westerns offer the best possibility of a native American subject matter in the movies.

Whitehall, Richard. "The Heroes are Tired." *Film Quarterly*, XX:2 (Winter, 1966–1967), 12–24. A rambling but fascinating study of the major themes in the historical development of Westerns. Beginning in the late 1940's Westerns took on greater complexity and began a process of self-examination.

Willett, Ralph. "The American Western: Myth and Anti-Myth." *Journal of Popular Culture*, IV:2 (Fall, 1970), 455–63. Westerns are appealing because they romanticize history, show the west as unspoiled paradise, articulate the individualist dream and visually treat law and violence questions. "New" Westerns are characterized by violence, degradation, moral complexity and a sense of history.

Woods, Frederick. "Hot Guns and Cold Women." *Films and Filming*, V (March, 1959), 11, 30. The falsification of the historic West, particularly in the depiction of gunfights and the stereotyping of women, give the Western much in common with the medieval romance.

Young, Vernon. "The West in Celluloid: Hollywood's Lost Horizons." *Southwest Review*, XXVIII (Spring, 1953), 126–34. Westerns are artistic failures because they have ignored history to create a false, simple-minded mythology. Includes short discussions of *The Ox-Bow Incident, Pursued, Red River, The Gunfighter, The Westerner* and *Destry Rides Again*.

Foreign Language Publications

Agel, Henri, ed. *Le Western*. Paris: Lettres Modernes, 1961.

Bazin, André. "Le Western." In his *Quest-ce que le cinéma*, Vol. III *Cinéma et Sociologie*. Paris: Editions de Cerf, 1961.

Bellour, Raymond and Patrick Brion, ed., *Le Western: sources, themes, mythologies auteurs, acteurs, filmographies.* Paris: Union Générale d'Editions, 1966.

Celluloide, No. 63 (March, 1963). A special issue on Westerns.

Chiattone, Antonio. *Il Film Western.* Milan: Poligono Società Editrice, 1949.

Cinéma 62, No. 68 (July–August, 1962). A special issue on Westerns.

Etudes Cinématographiques, Nos. 12 and 13. Paris: Minard, 1969.

Ford, Charles. *Histoire du Western.* Paris: Pierre Horay, 1964.

Kezich, Tulio, ed. *Il Western maggiorenne*: saggi e documenti sul film storico Americano. Trieste: F. Zigiotti, 1953.

Présence du cinéma, Nos. 2 and 3 (1959). A special issue on Westerns.

Rieupeyrout, Jean-Louis. *La grande aventure du Western.* Paris: Editions du Cerf, 1964. A revision of *Le Western.*

———. *Le Western*, Paris, 1953.

Periodicals

Classic Film Collector. 734 Philadelphia Street, Indiana, Pennsylvania 15701. Quarterly. Irregular short news notices of Western stars and films and a regular column on Westerns, "The Oaters," by Tom Brennen.

Film Collector's Registry. 10918 Sageburrow, Houston, Texas 77034. Monthly. Irregular interviews, news and features—usually short—about Westerns.

Filmograph. Murray Summers, Orlean, Virginia 22128. Quarterly. Occasional articles and filmographies on "B" Western performers.

Views and Reviews. 633 W. Wisconsin, Suite 1700, Milwaukee, Wisconsin 53203. Quarterly. In-depth articles on specific Western films. Also, occasional articles on Western performers, Western serials, etc. Emphasis is on detailed accuracy.

Wild West Stars. Jim Ward, Route 8, Thorngrove Pike, Knoxville, Tennessee 37914. Bi-monthly. Articles and columns on "B" Western stars, movie history, types of Westerns, etc., mostly of an appreciative nature but often quite detailed.

Western Film Collector. Western Film Collectors, P.O. Box 17059, Nashville, Tennessee 37217. Bi-monthly. Articles reviewing the careers of notable "B" Western performers. Emphasis on historical details, filmographies.

Western Star Digest. P.O. Box 12367, Nashville, Tennessee, 37212. Bi-monthly. Mostly short news notices and reproductions of publicity materials. Each issue devoted to a specific star or group. Of minimal use for serious study.

Index[1]

---

1 Index covers pages 1–128 only.